AF433370

FitzOmar's Rubaiyat and Its Interpretations

Edward FitzGerald's 'Rubaiyat of Omar Khayyam' poem stunned Victorian England soon after Darwin's 'Origin of the Species' had shocked their sensibilities, but soon they and the world came to embrace what came to be known as the greatest poem in history, and also the one most often illustrated.

Omar had the deep and grand ideas, but it was FitzGerald, as a kindred soul and poet, who dressed them in such fine clothes, attracting the world to them forever.

The synergy of FitzOmar takes us far and away from the mundane, everyday, low-life, blah-blah, sit-com type situations, into the glorious reaches of deeper thinking about the Big Questions, as well as to the great philosophical tenet of enjoying life to the fullest.

FitzGerald's transmogrification of Omar is near unbelievable in its excellence, one of those rare poetic products that could go on for hundreds of years without equal. Shelley was close, in his poem, 'Adonais', as well as was Thomas Gray, in 'An Elegy Written in a Country Church Yard'.

See the 'Concordance of the Rubáiyát' online to see from what very plain original language FitzGerald developed his stupendous quatrain gems time and time again. FitzGerald even discarded some quatrains because they were merely quite masterful instead of meeting the perfectly superb standard he had set for himself. I have restored them.

All things, roll on "impotently", by Omar. We are, as Shakespeare noted, but actors in a play, strutting and posturing. When were we ever responsible for how we were or are at any given moment?

The Rubaiyat Expanded

Copyright 2021 Austin P. Torney

(aka 'The Extended Rubaiyat of Omar Khayyam
Via Its Equal Interspersed')

YouTube Videos: MagicalVideos Channel

Dedication

*I dedicate the Rubaiyat's increase
To those who happily labored to tease
Beautiful meaning out of the plain verse,
With the rare insight to grant a new lease.*

Notation

Edward FitzGerald's quatrains are numbered: 1. — 115.
Austin's quatrains are in italics font. Those by Jennifer
or Positor are noted directly. Those quatrains remaining
were reworded from the Bodleian/Calcutta manuscripts.

Preface

*In this expanded Rubaiyat,
new Omaresque quatrains have
been inserted, many by Omar,
and many through Omar's spirit in Austin.*

*Many splendid quatrains are buried deep
In the manuscripts of Bodleian's keep
And in Calcutta's tome lost, long entombed,
Herein given life by enhancement's leap.*

*The verses beat the same, in measured chime.
Lines one-two set the stage, one-two-four rhyme.
Verse three's the pivot around which thought turns;
Line four delivers the sting, just in time.*

Introduction

Expanding The Rubaiyat was quite the ambitious undertaking and so only the best extensions would do:

1. The best versions from FitzGerald's Rubaiyat five editions have been chosen. I've inserted section titles.

2. Nine quatrains that FitzGerald removed have been restored and five quatrains from his notes have been added, making for a new total of 115 quatrains.

3. Quatrains from the Bodleian and Calcutta manuscripts were improved or rewritten and were inserted at the appropriate places.

4. Many of my own best omaresque quatrains were improved and inserted at the appropriate places.

5. Several Rubaiyat-related background themes are presented at the end, many of them containing quatrains:

   The Find of the Rubaiyat Edition Known as the 'Great Omar';

   The Secret Life of Omar's Rubaiyat Poems;

   On Poetry; Extra Quatrains;

   The Transmogrification From the Farsi Arabic;

   Omar's Other Works;

   Austin's New Calendar;

   The Answers to Everything.

What benefit to life then? I suggest it is Experience, which can be mostly a joy—with Omar's love, drink, food, friends, adventure, romance, and deep feeling, although transient, but ever of the glorious Now, and generally free of shame and blame, being in the Paradise of right here, plus we being just as organic as anything else in nature, and thus no more important, "willy-nilly blowing".

"Round which we Phantom Figures come and go" is about the noumena from which our phenomena arise from, as a kind of holo-graphic phantasmagorial realm of the "Magic Shadow-Show". What lies behind is difficult to get at, but there has been some progress, such as in-sights into our brain networks.

"The Eternal Saki from that Bowl has pour'd/Millions of Bubbles like us, and will pour" because, well, in short, it has to, all things happening over and over again for all time. It's Deja vu all over again.

"Which, for the Pastime of Eternity, He doth Himself contrive, enact, behold" and the like is that, if one plays along with the myth, it is like that He thought of, planned, designed, and implemented humans and their nature, with an inherent wide-ranging spectrum of ca-pacity for and from Good to Bad; however, in this myth-take 'God' bears no responsibility for His recipe express-ing itself in just the way He all-knowingly intended it to. Why His surprise and disappointment?

Often, big paradoxes mightily arrive when a proposed realm is declared 'invisible', and Omar is ever up to the task. Brave Omar knocks 'god' without fear.

When "You shall be You no more" and "And naked on the Air of Heaven ride", and the like, it is perhaps that there not really a redundant soul ever living on, made of some invisible angelic vapour that duplicates and preserves our brain neuron network, which readily maintains what is already you just fine, in some essence of an already evolutionarily expensively formed brain. FitzGerald's 'quicksilver' is either as the above soul or as wine coursing through us.

Omar cites the limits to Knowing Everything as us moving toward a carpe diem centering in the now. He writes "...evermore Came out by the same Door as in I went", "...But not the Master knot of Human Fate", and so forth. Not being able to know is the same dilemma facing his Impotent Great Wheel itself.

And so Omar unveils his basic human philosophy for the human condition, the central tenet being the primacy of the 'Now'— over "Unborn To-morrow and dead Yesterday".

> The Moving Finger writes; and, having writ,
> Moves on: nor all thy Piety nor Wit
> Shall lure it back to cancel half a Line,
> Nor all thy Tears wash out a Word of it.

While the above probably refers to predestination by Allah, as made more explicit in other quatrains, it can also relate now-a-days to more scientifically modern views as to how each moment arises in Time, in the Now, and then completely passes away, wholly replaced right then and there by the next Now, which process, or even 'processing', can't be stopped, much like the deterministic chain "That none can slip, nor break, nor over-reach".

Whether there is being or becoming, as eternalism or presentism, is still an open question. We don't know the mode of time, for either mode would have the same appearance to us.

What one did long ago is done, dead, and gone, obviating any real shame and blame, but one must as well give up any fame, as well, crediting all to Fate. Plus, indeed, can anyone really be held responsible for who/what they've come to be from nature and nurture?

While Omar rails against a predestination by 'God', it is for other, godless, reasons that determinism might still be much the way events have to be, but for some possible quantum level randomness, if any, which damages the will, anyway, harming it, not helping it at all, as much as we somehow wish to think that our will can be free of itself or that we or any part of physical Nature can do the same to somehow be self-made entities as mini first causes. It seems that for one to have 'God', whatever Nature does is what 'God' does, and so thus 'god' is not required.

Omar reveals that an ultimate basis without Origin, such as his causeless Great Wheel. standing in for the Eternal Basis, cannot even know its own reason for existence, and is powerless over this and its state, with no choice given to it for its being, it having to do just what it does and naught else, much as we may also have to admit to at our level.

"It rolls impotently on as Thou or I", or it just 'IS', ever and eternal, without a beginning or end, and what never begins cannot have a certain direction, design, meaning, or purpose put to it in the first place that never was.

> Whose secret Presence through Creation's veins
> Running Quicksilver-like eludes your pains;
> Taking all shapes from Máh to Máhi and
> They change and perish all—but He remains;

Thanks to you both, Edward FitzGerald and Omar Khayyam, for the insights, as well as for attending to the serious task of pointing out the dubious and the deep.

THE AWAKENING

1.

AWAKE! For Morning in the Bowl of Night
Has flung the Stone that puts the Stars to Flight:
And Lo! the Hunter of the East has caught
The Sultan's Turret in a Noose of Light.

The sun doth smite the roofs with Orient ray
And, Khosrau like, his wine-red sheen display:
Arise, and drink! the herald of the dawn
Uplifts his voice, and cries, 'Oh, drink to-day!'

2.

Dreaming when Dawn's Left Hand was in the Sky
I heard a Voice within the Tavern cry,
"Awake, my Little ones, and fill the Cup
Before Life's Liquor in its Cup be dry."

The universe's mantle binds us worn—
Tears feeding the river on which we're borne.
Hell's but an ember of our senseless fears;
Heaven's the rose-breath of opening morn.

A dream spoke to me, while I slumbered deep,
"You're wasting on the threshold of Death's keep;
Doth in repose does the rosebud blossom?
Entombed, you can for eternity sleep."

At this hour of the dawning; up, flower of thy kind!
With rubies in crystal, come gladden the mind;
For this moment we borrow from Time on the wing
Full oft wilt thou seek nor again wilt thou find.

Angel of joyful foot! the dawn is nigh;
Pour wine, and lift your tuneful voice on high,
Sing how Jamshyds and Khosraus bit the dust,
Whelmed by the rolling months, from Tir to Dai!

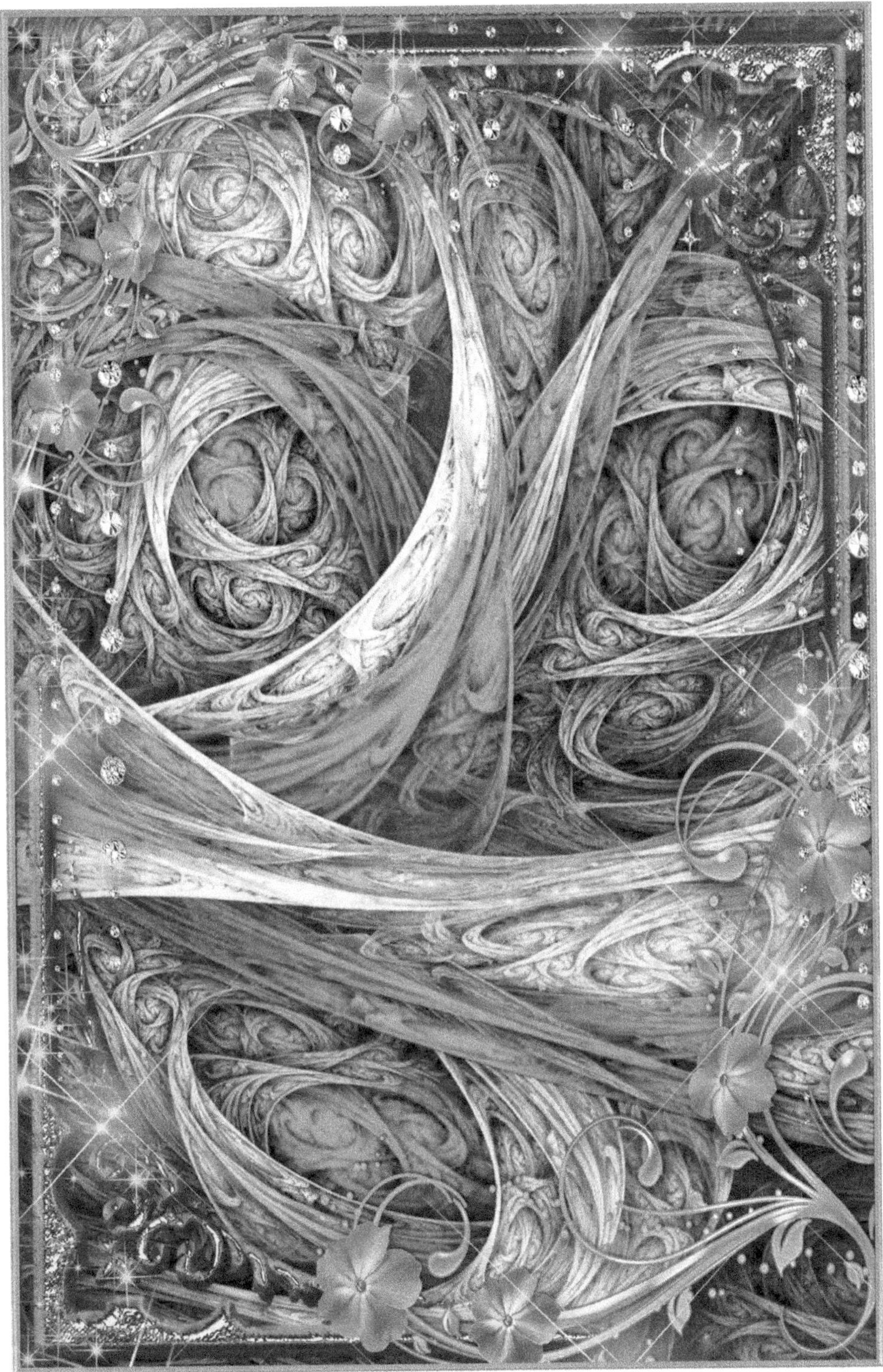

3.

And, as the Cock crew, those who stood before
The Tavern shouted—"Open then the Door.
You know how little while we have to stay,
And, once departed, may return no more."

Oh! wine is richer that the realm of Jam,
More fragrant than the food of Miriam;
Sweeter are sighs that drunkards heave at morn
Than strains of Bu Sa'id and Bin Adham.

To Solitude Retired

4.

Now the New Year reviving old Desires,
The thoughtful Soul to Solitude retires,
Where the White Hand Of Moses on the Bough
Puts out, and Jesus from the Ground suspires.

Aft the cloud's eyes water the soil that dried,
The sun's warm breath wakes up the seeds inside;
Hence, all the plants, trees, and flowers revive,
And over mead, stream, and wayside preside.

The Spirit breathes life with its holy might;
Spring blossoms replace winter's snowy white;
Cloudy vapors coalesce into drops;
The airs the lovers with fragrance invite.

Spring kisses the earth, leaving flowers there,
Like those whose perfume first scented virgin air,
As again, the fragrant glen, in Heaven's prayer,
Hails Earth's anniversary with flowers fair.

Slake love's thirst for life's earthly endeavor
Near a stream where wildflowers grow forever.
Flowers influence our feelings—deep they roam:
Flora's fairest flowers compose Heaven's poem.

Our souls to solitude often retire,
When the noise of life sets the nerves on fire.
Here the rhythmic songs of nature inspire;
We sense the vibrance of an inner choir.

5.

Iram indeed is gone with all its Rose,
And Jamshyd's Sev'n-ring'd Cup where no one knows;
But still the Vine her ancient Ruby yields,
And still a Garden by the Water blows.

And Lo! King Jamshyd's Golden Garden Land
Now's the sunken Atlantis of his band.
A turret reaches forth, yet sinks in a
Rolling dune—life's but a handful of sand!

The concave mirror of a telescope
Is as Jam's world-reflecting bowl or globe:
Beyond the seven-ringed celestials,
The Secrets of the Cosmos are unveiled.

Jamschid reigned seven hundred years, wary;
Karum, the rich gold-maker, lies buried,
With all his treasures, near the Pyramids;
Kai Kaus' palace was built by demons varied.

Jewry hath seen a thousand prophets die,
Sinai a thousand Musas mount the sky;
How many Caesars Rome's proud forum crossed!
'Neath Wasra's dome how many monarchs lie!

6.

And David's Lips are lock't; but in divine
High piping Pelevi, with "Wine! Wine! Wine!
Red Wine!"—the Nightingale cries to the Rose
That sallow Cheek of hers to'incarnadine.

The morn has bloomed, the warm day's growing lush;
Past, the garden's dust run from the rain's gush.

And Lo! King Jamshyd's Golden Garden Land
Now's the sunken Atlantis of his band.
A turret reaches forth, then sinks in a
Rolling dune—life's but a handful of sand!

Wine's nightingale sings in tongue to the drooped:
Oh, pale rose, we both must drink to blush toward flush!

The Rose's skirt reveals, shorn by the breeze,
And Nightingales rejoice her in the trees;
Let us lay about the rose bush with ease,
For many have turned to dust just like these.

Drink the lifeblood of the grapes you've sown,
Before pressing time squeezes out thy own.
Do toast with thy chalice and all inspire:
'To life's red wine I give all that I own!'

For my sins of spring I repent my part;
No! I mustn't atone, for how, apart,
Could I resist the beauty of love's truth
When roses and tulips bloom in love's heart?

Oh meddling thoughts that harp on reason's plea,
My cheeks glow red from the loved one's grape tree,
So to your face I throw my other hand,
And drop you into sleep, oh fantasy.

THE INVITATION

7.

Come, fill the Cup, and in the Fire of Spring
The Winter Garment of Repentance fling:
The Bird of Time has but a little way
To fly—and Lo! the Bird is on the Wing.

A moment of eternity in hand,
Caught from a wingéd creature on time's sand,
Yet put aside to later view in peace.
It flies! Now pursue it through Never-Land.

Some may ask of Life: "How does one find love?"
Life says, "Be still! Don't rush far and above;

Stop; let love's butterfly alight on you,
For that's the touch that romance is made of."

Spring's New Year unfolds the garden's jewels:
The sweet rose, my Peri, and April Fools.
Yester-now expires gifting the present;
'Twould be naught to speak outside of what rules.

The morn springs us o'er oblivion's brink,
The stars overcome, sunk in the day's drink.
We race our paths, past Allah's golden dome,
Unto the green-grassed river-bank to sink.

Those who dally on the soft river ,
Drinking an houri's morning breath, alas,
While the flowered Persia fumes waft about,
Are free and saved from the mosque's tiring mass.

On spring's green bank, my houri drinks with me,
Pouring love's cup into our souls thirsty;
Would I then gasp for Heaven's Paradise,
Then, I daresay, dogs whine better than me.

For those who see, grass and stream meet the eyes,
In forest and desert, where Heav'n's realm lies,
And there, life's Hell has gone away, you'd say,
As you consort with maids of Paradise.

Heart to my hand to lift the glass of wine;
Hand to heart to hold the houri of mine.
Dullards say, "Repent of thy overflow."
Ha, I will none of it; I'm my own vine.

When morning breaks, the rosy cup drain,
And dash fame's crystal on the rocks again;
Thy lute is sweet, thy tresses soft as down;
Heaven is here, and future glory vain.

8.
Whether at Naishapur or Babylon,
Whether the Cup with sweet or bitter run,
The Wine of Life keeps oozing drop by drop,
The Leaves of Life keep falling one by one.

From life we oft drew wine, now dregs to drink,
Once flaunted silk, but now in tatters shrink;
Such changes wisdom holds of slight account
To those who stand on death's appalling brink!

9.
And look—a thousand Blossoms with the Day
Woke—and a thousand scatter'd into Clay:
And this first Summer Month that brings the Rose
Shall take Jamshyd and Kaikobád away.

When showers of Spring the tulips' cheeks overflow
Arise and to the wine-cup haste to go,
For this green where thou sport'st to-day, perchance
On some near morrow from thy dust may grow.

She grows a clutch of blossoms to propose;
His zephyr blows nature's page to disclose:
Spring, departing, caresses the summer—
From their only kiss blooms the lovely rose.

Spring's last breath awakens him—he's living:
The life-force passes to summer from spring—
His clover spreads, vines grow strong, roses cling,
All from the kiss of which she died giving.

10.
But come with old Khayyam, and leave the Lot
Of Kaikobád and Kaikhosrú forgot:
Let Rustum cry "To Battle" as he likes
Or Hatim Tai cry Supper—heed them not.

Old wine betters Kai's kingdom's palace new,
And far does it his golden throne outdo.
The cup a hundred times beats all realms, and
The wine-jar lid bests the crown of Khosrau.

So much sweeter sounds are one's lover's sighs
Than the groan of war that wins great prize.
One taste of love's dear wine by far out-buys
A Sultan's wealth in some rich paradise.

THE VERSE IN THE WILDERNESS

11.

With me along some Strip of Herbage strown
That just divides the Desert from the sown,
Where name of Slave and Sultan scarce is known,
And pity Sultan Máhmud on his Throne.

Who knew that the twin-born Peri was bred
From lower flesh and higher spirit bled,
Where the Hellish desert meets the greensward,
When the hot sands and the luscious turf wed.

Follow the path, past the rose bushes sight,
Where the forest opens to a shaft of light.
Here the flower beds, one with a lush of grass,
Where greenish light glows forth the hours we'll pass.

Here the purest pitch, where the bluebirds sing,
Where the lilacs ne'er know it isn't spring,
Where Heaven's eternity bides its time,
Where all woes and troubles have taken wing.

Here the grape vines ne'er toll their final knell;
E'er they pour ruby nectar in life's dell,
An idyll, where we're the cups to be filled
To the brim, to spill, quenched and drenched so well.

One wine draught out-buys a Shah's paradise,
All the sparkling jewels of the skies,
And China's Kingdom—trifles unneeded;
What bitter drink beats a thousand sweets' prize!

Where the river runs, far from Sultan's throne,
We live by the stream-side, just us alone.
Here we've the perfect equilibrium:
Poor but rich, home yet free, great but unknown.

12.

A Book of Verses underneath the Bough,
A Jug of Wine, a Loaf of Bread—and Thou
Beside me singing in the Wilderness—
Oh, Wilderness were Paradise enow!

Though hewn for study of the stars I am,
And philosophy, too, hear Old Khayyam:
Best her tangled tresses attract your view;
Then enjoy wine, verse, and a leg of lamb.

Have we gourds, bread, and a leg of mutton,
While writing verse in the wilderness, yon,
Oh tulip-cheeks, lovelier than the moon,
It treats beyond the bounds of a Sultan.

We choose the love nest over greed's estates,
With romance, bread, wine, and verse as our traits,
Heart and soul buy poverty's privacy;
Rich is the fortune that poorness creates.

Cast from thy glory that hindering veil,
Rather than give up thy body and fail;
Wear instead the old rug of poverty,
And thus the same as a Sultan prevail.

13.

Some for the Glories of This World; and some
Sigh for the Prophet's Paradise to come;

Ah, take the Cash, and let the Credit go,
Nor heed the rumble of a distant Drum!

In Heaven, the pleasure drums beat like rain,
Or so 'tis claimed, to relieve mortal pain;
But, we needn't pay for promise beyond:
Here, from life's currency, we've the same!

14.
Were it not Folly, Spider-like to spin
The Thread of present Life away to win—
What? for ourselves, who know not if we shall
Breathe out the very Breath we now breathe in!

To future columns we stretch our present row,
By a lifeline of tenuously spun vow.
Oh, how soon the weighted web begins to fail;
The only real time under our feet is now.

Life's a web, of whos, whys, whats, and hows,
Stretched as time between eternal boughs.
Gossamer threads bear the beads that glisten,
Each moment a sequence of instant nows.

No matter how one tries to shake from boughs
The fruits of truth from the Tree of Knows;
Computation makes not yet the morrows;
There's naught else but lone, resultant Nows.

Quatrains are the pearls strung along the wrath,
Illuminating beads that love's web hath,
Lighting the decades of life's rosary,
To thread the enchanted gossamer path.

Days are the cyclic units of time's pearls—
Beads worn round in the necklace of the months;
They distance themselves, like night echoes,
Into the rosary of the seasons.

Memory's ideas recall the last heard tone;
Sensation savors what is presently known;
Imagination anticipates coming sounds;
The delight is such that none could produce alone.

THE BLOWING ROSE

15.
Look to the Rose that blows about us—"Lo,
Laughing," she says, "into the World I blow:
At once the silken Tassel of my Purse
Tear, and its Treasure on the Garden throw."

Each morning, dewdrops pearl the tulip's face,
While the violet drooping bows in grace,
But, fairest, the rosebud, does closely lace
Her skirt to shield her blush from wind's abase.

A rose's prime lasts for but an hour of morn:
Flowering and free, then fragile and forlorn,
The petals float to earth, and there signify
That beauty's past, for all that's left is the thorn.

At first, we sleep in our dear mother's womb;
At last, we sleep in the cold silent tomb.
In between, Life whispers a dream that says,
Wake, live, for the rose withers all too soon!

With the Rose the Earth is rich forever—
It's born from spring's dying kiss to summer;
It wears all the gems the dew has wreathed,
Blooming wherever summer's breath has breathed.

The rose has thorns to keep the beasts away;
As such they preserve her fragrant bouquet.
Her petals unfold, meeting the light of day—
The queen of flowers melts my heart away.

Like the moon, challenge night and gain the light;
Like the rose, suffer the thorn—gain the fragrance;
Of life, surrender to live forever—
Enlightened more than a thousand suns.

16.

The Worldly Hope men set their Hearts upon
Turns Ashes—or it prospers; and anon,
Like Snow upon the Desert's dusty Face
Lighting a little Hour or two—is gone.

In the hourglass of time, the desert's grains
Ever blow, grind, and blast the camel trains;
Yet, where the river flows, where grasses blow,
You and I, beloved, drink the wine's remains.

17.

And those who husbanded the Golden Grain,
And those who flung it to the Winds like Rain,
Alike to no such aureate Earth are turn'd
As, buried once, Men want dug up again.

Ere Fate fells you dried up like an old leaf,
Course red wine through thy veins of life so brief.
Ne'er for treasured gold will you be dug up,
Nor even sought by an impoverished thief.

Ah! Wheel of Heaven to tyranny inclined,
'Twas e'er your wont to show yourself unkind;
And, cruel earth, if they should cleave your breast.
What store of buried jewels they would find!

Ere fate on thee fall like a thief in the gloom.
Call for wine of the hue of the rose in full bloom.
Art thou gold, O thou heedless know-nothing, that thee
They should bury and after dig up from earth's womb?

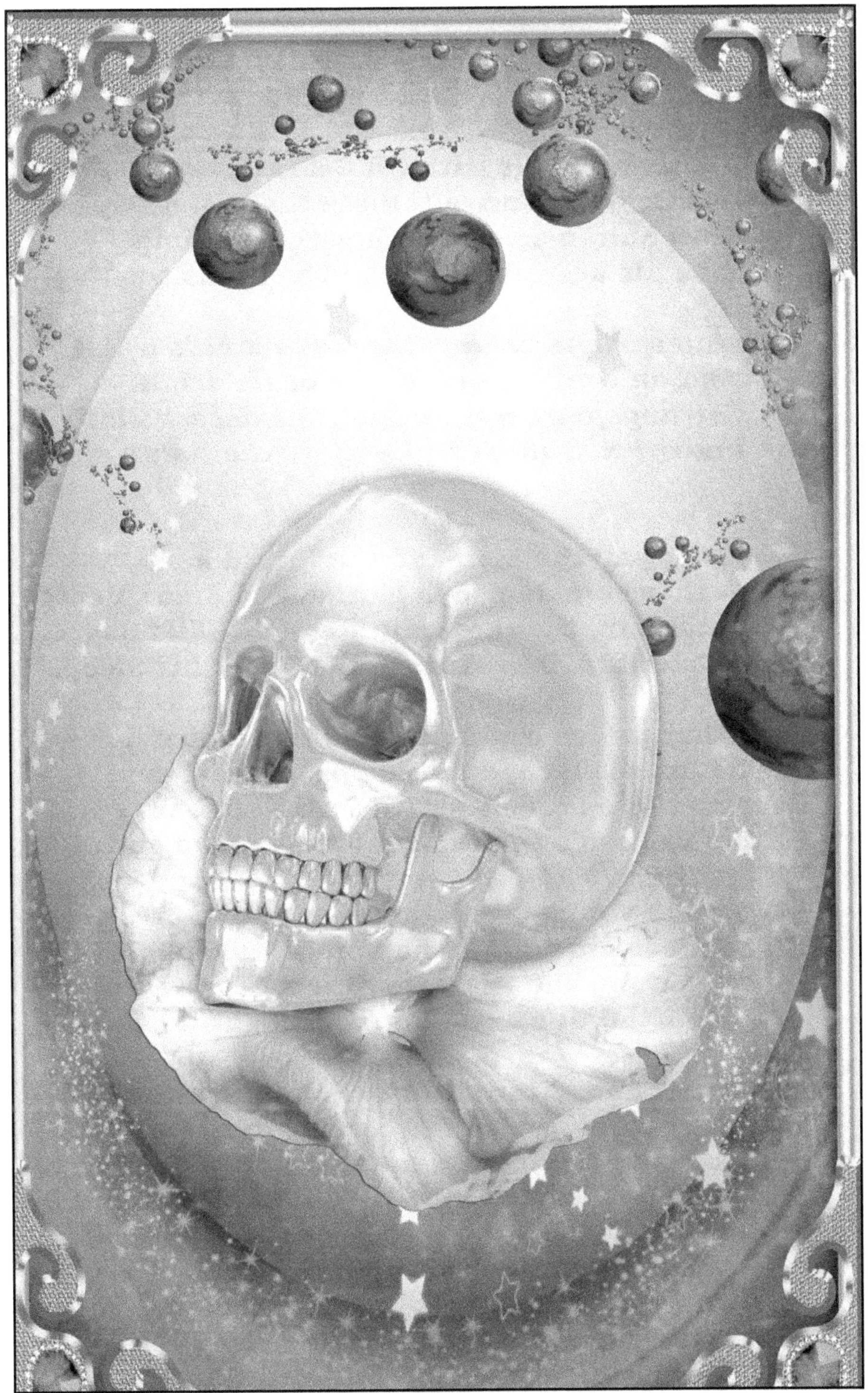

THE COURTS OF JAMSHYD

18.
Think, in this batter'd Caravanserai
Whose Doorways are alternate Night and Day,
How Sultan after Sultan with his Pomp
Abode his destin'd Hour, and went his way.

Morning springs us over the wasteland's brink,
And on time's sand we the oasis drink.
Life's strange caravan through the desert winds,
Back toward Nothing; drink—afore the lights sink.

19.
They say the Lion and the Lizard keep
The courts where Jamshyd gloried and drank deep:
And Bahrám, that great Hunter—the Wild Ass
Stamps o'er his Head, but cannot break his Sleep.

In that palace which Bahram took the cup,
The fox whelped, and the lion took its sup;
Bahram there brought death to the wild ass gur;
Now Bahram's been taken by the grave gur.

Where in yon palace Bahram wine-cup prest.
The roe bears young, the lion oft takes rest.
King Bahram who in noose oft caught the Gur,
See how the Gur hath Bahram caught at last!

The Great Equalizer stalks all creatures made,
Lying ever just 'round the corner, in the shade,
Taking both human and the beetle as one,
After their lives are spent from rolling some dung.

What is the world? A caravanserai,
A piebald pavilion of night and day;
A feast whereat a thousand Jamshyds sat,
A couch whereon a thousand Bahrams lay.

20.

The Palace that to Heav'n his pillars threw,
And Kings the forehead on his threshold drew—
I saw the solitary Ringdove there,
And "Coo, coo, coo," she cried; and "Coo, coo, coo."

I saw a bird perched on the walls of Tus,
Before him lay the skull of Kai Kawus,
And thus he made his moan, "Alas, poor king!
Thy drums are hushed, thy 'larums have rung truce."

E'en our smoke from ember's ash fades away,
That warp of our woof and weave burned to clay.
How many beautiful hearts have melted here?
Where in heaven's cosmic vault wefts their sway?

THE RIVER LIP

21.

Ah! my Beloved, fill the Cup that clears
To-Day of past Regrets and future Fears-
To-morrow?—Why, To-morrow I may be
Myself with Yesterday's Sev'n Thousand Years.

Engraved is 'The End' of your earthly sigh;
Six sides surround: five are dirt, one is sky.
Shov'ling, Death speaks to you at last, and asks,
What were you doing during all of nigh?'

22.

For some we loved, the loveliest and the best
That from his Vintage rolling Time has prest,
Have drunk their Cup a Round or two before,
And one by one crept silently to Rest.

In spring, we rise from the garden in birth.
Summer blooms long with the roses' fresh mirth

Autumn creeps in, we wither on the vine.
Last comes winter, when we return to earth.

23.
And we, that now make merry in the Room
They left, and Summer dresses in new Bloom,
    Ourselves must we beneath the Couch of Earth
Descend, ourselves to make a Couch—for whom?

24.
I sometimes think that never blows so red
The Rose as where some buried Caesar bled;
    That every Hyacinth the Garden wears
Dropt in its Lap from some once lovely Head.

Over the Ruler's tomb bleeds Beauty's rose,
As the tulip's blood cups the Truth that knows,
    While the violet's marked Goodness grows—
Love's braid untwined to us in spring disclosed.

Sung songs of life composed now lie reposed,
Thy face-dust Beauty's music decomposed;
Ah, Sun's Venus-brows we're honored to brush,
That future's wand will rearrange recomposed.

25.
And this delightful Herb whose tender Green
Fledges the River's Lip on which we lean—
    Ah, lean upon it lightly! for who knows
From what once lovely Lip it springs unseen!

The thorn that bends 'neath every creature's tread,
May spring from some love's curl, fair brow of maid,
    And every tile on palace battlement
Some Vizier's finger be or Sultan's head!

Sung songs of life composed now lie reposed,
Thy face-dust Beauty's music decomposed;

THE LONG REST

26.
Ah, make the most of what we yet may spend,
Before we too into the Dust Descend;
Dust into Dust, and under Dust, to lie,
Sans Wine, sans Song, sans Singer and—sans End!

THEOLOGY

27.
Alike for those who for To-Day prepare,
And those that after some To-Morrow stare,
A Muezzin from the Tower of Darkness cries
"Fools! your Reward is neither Here nor There."

Some look for truth in creeds, and forms, and rules;
Some grope for doubts or dogmas in the schools;
But from behind the veil a voice proclaims,
"Your road lies neither here nor there, O fools."

Let not the certainty of the present be
Held mortgage for the Deed of Futurity,
For tomorrow's just a gleam from afar
And yesterday's but a cold ash of thee.

Not quite sober blessed nor drunk to excess;
Never too foolish nor very reckless—
Ah, life's passion is so reasonable
In this delicate state of awareness.

Classicists drone toward dull perfection;
Romanticists drown in feeling's affection;
Worse, others alternate between extremes;
It's not this nor that, but of joined direction.

If Fortune leads you to her masquerade,
Beware of the sweet desserts therein laid,
For, once lured by poison's sandy mirage,
Envenomed, you can't thwart the saber's blade.

28.

Oh, come with old Khayyam, and leave the Wise
To talk; one thing is certain, that Life flies;
One thing is certain, and the Rest is Lies;
The Flower that once has blown for ever dies.

We pick some Dandelions ripe enough
To have gone from gold to just so much fluff,
Reminding us, when soft blown with a puff,
That time will spread us too amid the dust.

Sweet is the breath of Spring to rose's face,
And thy sweet face adds charm to this fair place;
To-day is sweet, but yesterday is sad,
And sad all mention of its parted grace.

The rose of which we so sweetly sing
Rises abloom in the joyous spring,
As a sprout from the soil of nature's earth,
In a grand, gloried, and triumphant birth.

On the first day that the summer blushes,
It blossoms red, as spring vanishes,
From its one and only kiss to summer.
Then the summer rose reigns, near forever,

Its tearing petals falling, from its toil,
Enriching the potpourri of the soil.

And laughs with the mirth of the long season sent,
Somewhere between happiness and contentment.
Golden autumn slowly creeps into the scene,
And then the autumnal rose withers, lean...

Then comes the winter seen, shutting the scene.
That's the living life of the rose that thrives.
The flower that once has blown forever dies.
What then, is the name of the rose?

We are the rose.

29.

Why, all the Saints and Sages who discuss'd
Of the Two Worlds so learnedly, are thrust
Like foolish Prophets forth; their Words to Scorn
Are scatter'd, and their Mouths are stopt with Dust.

The sages who have compassed sea and land,
Their secret to search out, and understand—
My mind misgives me if they ever solve
The scheme on which this universe is planned.

THE SAME DOOR

30.

Myself when young did eagerly frequent
Doctor and Saint, and heard great Argument
About it and about: but evermore
Came out by the same Door as in I went.

We've approached the Mystery, and have found
That Beginnings can't be, so what goes round
Must be all things, as there's no point to impart
A design; yet drink—to naught more we're bound!

Be wide aware when chance shines as your sun,
For she in turn happens on everyone.
Graciously welcome the lady of luck,
By recognizing her as Dame Fortune.

WHENCE AND WHITHER

31.
With them the Seed of Wisdom did I sow,
And with my own hand labour'd it to grow:
And this was all the Harvest that I reap'd—
"I came like Water, and like Wind I go."

32.
Into this Universe, and why not knowing,
Nor whence, like Water willy-nilly flowing:
And out of it, as Wind along the Waste,
I know not whither, willy-nilly blowing.

Time on its stream brings all sweet things to us;
Water of life; we drink time, it drinks us!
This aqua-vita quenches human thirst.
Time on its stream bears all sweet things from us.

33.
What, without asking, hither hurried whence?
And, without asking, whither hurried hence!
Another and another Cup to drown
The Memory of this Impertinence!

Hither unto this fair Earth I was bred,
The Cosmos' reflection not more ahead,
And hence forth, my splendour rent asunder,
Yet to my ears the point remains unsaid.

I asked not, but became, whither blowing,
My hither going veiled to my knowing,
Hence thither I must live on wine glowing,
Absolved of worries, so freely flowing.

Worries may not come true, and if they do,
Thus they would, and then in them you must stew.

Past imperfect points to a future tense,
Yet ever only Nows does the Wheel brew.

What shall be, remedy or pain, or mix?
No contest, for we're wise to change's tricks,
And can expect sorrow and joy alike;
But, who cares! They'll pass; we all go to bricks.

On to the tavern we creep, its drinks calling,
Where the inquisitive sit, pondering.
One and another says, "We've some questions,
For we've all been born here without asking."

VAIN QUESTIONING

34.

Up from Earth's Center through the Seventh Gate
I rose, and on the Throne of Saturn sate,
And many Knots unravel'd by the Road;
But not the Master-knot of Human Fate.

The circling orbs that in the night skies abound
Do the minds of the learned ones confound.
Dare not loosen the grasp of wisdom's thread;
Even the wise grow faint from the whirls around.

All from stardust begins and ends in thee.
The mighty wrecks of the elements are strewn
Across the universe, like chaff from the harvest,
Much of the Cosmos still a vast wasteland.

Since there's no lasting abode on this sphere,
'Tis folly wine and loves away to steer;
Oh most boring belaborer of creeds,
What matters those realms neither there nor here.

How long shall we be flushed, untying knots?
What boots if Fate long life, or short, allots?

Pour out thy cup of life's wine, as we'll all
Become, under the workshop, earthen pots.

35.
There was a Door to which I found no Key:
There was a Veil past which I could not see:
Some little Talk awhile of Me and Thee
There was—and then no more of Thee and Me.

Think not that I am existent as 'I',
Or talk the talk and walk the walk of 'I',
For all's of the 'IS'; the Cosmos is I;
Where then, and what, who, and whence is this 'I'?

Eterne's transitions doom forms' permanence;
But the time required for their constructance
Restrains for a while the shapes' destructance;
Thus they can slowly traverse life's distance.

Heaven's Great Wheel e'er whirls its energy,
It having to turn and return, to be,
Transmuting, as ne'er still—eternally,
Into life's temporary pattern trees.

Each holds within itself the seed of the other:
Yin reaches climax then retreats in Yang's favor—
Cyclic movement of rotational symmetry.
Rounded life is the blend of Yin-Yang together.

36.
Earth could not answer; nor the Seas that mourn
In flowing Purple, of their Lord Forlorn;
Nor rolling Heaven, with all his Signs reveal'd
And hidden by the sleeve of Night and Morn.

"Bless your soul with tongues of fire; Holy Spirit burn;
Leave no trace of man's desire; Holy Spirit turn."
Oh, man, why detest thy constitution;
Doth thou think Nature has a lot to learn?

"Where am I going? Am I important?"
You're going nowhere; here is your life's plant.
"In the mosque, they say 'God' as if it's true."
'Faith' in their wishes is behind what they chant.

"The preachers claim 'perhaps' as fact and truth."

Their ingrained beliefs the priests' duly preach,
As if notions were truth and fact to teach.
Oh, cleric, repent; at least say, 'Have faith';
Yet, of unknowns ne'er shown none can e'er reach.

How long will they prate of eternity?
Why proclaim as sure some uncertainty?
'Tis yon the cape of man's ability.
To unlock every door, wine's the key.

So Nature got it wrong, the pious say,
In man's constitution, erring its essay,
Granting so many ways to go astray;
Well, then, Who, do they say, penned this world's play?

37.

Then to the rolling Heav'n itself I cried,
Asking, "What Lamp had Destiny to guide
Her little Children stumbling in the Dark?"
And—"A blind understanding!" Heav'n replied.

Why do we wander around in the dark,
In the middle of the night like this?
Well, if we knew the answer to that one,
We would have been home some hours ago.

Do we not tire, e'er walking, looking, lame?
At first, we did, yes, yet life's beauty came:
The grand moment of wings grown; lifting, new.
The rhythm flies us—our music plays through.

THE SOUL OF THE CUP

38.
Then to Lip of this poor earthen Urn
I lean'd, the secret Well of Life to learn:
And Lip to Lip it murmur'd—"While you live,
Drink!—for once dead you never shall return."

39.
I think the Vessel, that with fugitive
Articulation answer'd, once did live,
And merry-make; and the cold Lip I kiss'd
How many Kisses might it take—and give.

I embrace the jug with joy and heart's burn
Of Elixir's secret wellspring to learn;
As kissed, it kisses back, and says, with its tongue,
"Drink, for once turned never will you return."

Seize the moment or lose its momentum,
Wearing time as a royal diadem;
Richly accelerate life's momentous gem,
Letting your motto be 'Carpe Diem'.

THE HEAVENLY POTTER

40.
For in the Market-place, one Dusk of Day,
I watch'd the Potter thumping his wet Clay:
And with its all obliterated Tongue
It murmur'd—"Gently, Brother, gently, pray!"

41.
And has not such a Story from of Old
Down Man's successive generations roll'd
Of such a clod of saturated Earth
Cast by the Maker into Human mold?

At the graven yard in Naishàpùr, I see
Blossoms in the dirt, blown from the rose tree.
As I dust my shoes, the clay speaks to me:
"Once I was like you; tread softly on me."

This jug did once, like me, love's sorrows taste,
And bonds of beauty's tresses once embraced,
This handle, which you see upon its side,
Has many a time twined round a slender waist.

This jug with whose arm I entwine my own,
Was too of stardust strewn and outward blown,
And may have once snuggled a lover kissed,
Neck on neck, a hand on her bosom thrown.

Last night my cup I smote against a stone.
Low was the act, my head with wine was flown.
The cup cried out to me in mystic tone,
"I was like thee, my fate will be thine own."

THE CUP OF LOVE

42.
Ah, fill the Cup:—what boots it to repeat
How Time is slipping underneath our Feet:
Unborn To-Morrow and dead Yesterday,
Why fret about them if To-day be sweet!

Together we sing in a fugal voice,
For we live in two-part harmonic choice.
We're opposite twins in love, a canon
Of chime in which we in unison rejoice.

Our fugal voices blend, part, join, and long
Weave in and out, the music sweeping strong,
And onward, upward, inward, and outward,
Until being is left to the spirit's song.

Like voices merged in the Canon Pachelbel,
We speak as one, as the knell to the bell,
You saying what I think and vice-versa,
In tune, in unison, yet parallel.

43.

And not a drop that from our Cups we throw
For Earth to drink of, but may steal below
To quench the fire of Anguish in some Eye
There hidden—far beneath, and long ago.

44.

As then the Tulip for her wonted sup
Of Heav'nly Vintage lifts her chalice up,
Do you, twin offspring of the soil, till Heav'n
To Earth invert you—like an empty Cup.

45.

Do you, within your little Hour of Grace,
The waving Cypress in your Arms enlace,
Before the Mother back into her Arms
Fold, and dissolve you in a last Embrace.

Rend the veil of sorrows shrouding thy face,
And shear the cloth of grief's idling chase;
Feast on her lips, wine, and verse; drain life's bank,
Ere Earth enfold thee in her breast's embrace.

46.

And if the Wine you drink, the Lip you press,
End in the Nothing all Things end in—Yes-
Then fancy while Thou art, Thou art but what
Thou shalt be—Nothing—Thou shalt not be less.

Pretend you're dead—gone, sitting on a star,
And regretting there an empty memoir...
"If only I might live it all again!"
Well, you're alive; so smile, because you are.

Persia-Fume
Fumes of Ageless Rhymes From Ancient Times
Remade into Victorian Perfume

THE CUP OF DEATH

47.

So when the Angel of the darker Drink
At last shall find you by the River-brink,
And, offering his Cup, Invite your Soul
Forth to your Lips to quaff—you shall not shrink.

I, as all, must one day soft surrender,
When the Angel knocks to take me under.
What will remain are my written quatrains—
For all those who'll come to be to ponder.

I fear not to pay the debt lent from death,
As here I'd not be if not for the breath
Extinguished in those who lived before;
Receive my future's deed and none the less.

THE ETERNAL SAKI

48.

And fear not lest Existence closing your
Account, and mine, should know the like no more;
The Eternal Saki from that Bowl has pour'd
Millions of Bubbles like us, and will pour.

Yet worry you that this Cosmos is the last,
That the likes of us will become the past,
Space wondering whither whence we went
After the last of us her life has spent?

The Eternal Saki has formed trillions of baubles
Like ours, for e'er—the comings and passings
Of which it ever emits to immerse
In the universal bubbles blown and burst.

So fear not that a debit close your
Account and mine, knowing the like no more;
The Eternal Source from its pot has pour'd
Zillions of bubbles like ours, and will pour.

What though the sky with its blue canopy
Doth close us in so that we can not see,
In the etern Cupbearer's wine methinks
There float a myriad bubbles like to me.

So, as thus thou lives on yester's credit line,
In nowhere's midst, now in this life of thine,
As of its bowl our cup of brew is mixed
Into the state of being that's called 'mine'.

Behind the Veil, being that which e'er thrives,
The Eternal 'IS' has ever been alive,
For that which hath no onset cannot die,
Nor a point from which to have any guide.

Whatever is eternal and is so well defined
Could never be as so, for it was never defined
In the first place, for that there never was
To define all that it forever did and does.

What 'IS' never began; it's the causeless,
For you can't get anything from none-ness;
Yet, there's a zero-sum balance of things,
Since still naught to make the things of, no less.

We are the beings of the everlasting light dream,
As products time and time again, by its means,
Of the eternal return, as baubles blown and burst,
Though draughts of time that quench life's thirst.

49.

When You and I behind the Veil are past,
Oh, but the long, long while the World shall last,

Which of our Coming and Departure heeds
As much as Ocean of a pebble-cast.

We clutch the skirt of Heaven, on it borne,
While the stars that go are at night reborn.
If Allah lives, and grants us a fresh morn,
We may one day the universe's dress adorn.

The raindrop falls and returns to the sea;
Dust floats to earth and merges with the lea;
Lives come and go in time—what's denoted?
Nows spark and fly; they've no eternity.

The drop wept for his severance from the sea,
But the sea smiled, for 'I am all,' said he,
'The Truth is all, nothing exists beside,
That one point circling apes plurality.'

Thy nature's knit by breath or fancies;
Be happy if imposed on you, that is ail;
Sit thou with wise and see that 'I' and 'thou'
Is grain of dust, a spark, a drop, and gale.

A reflected bird crosses the glassy sky,
And passes water lilies floating on high,
While waves ripple the leaves of mirrored trees.
We meet at the looking-glass when days die.

50.

One Moment in Annihilation's Waste,
One moment, of the Well of Life to taste—
The Stars are setting, and the Caravan
Draws to the dawn of Nothing—Oh, make haste!

Morning springs thee over the wasteland's brink,
And on time's sand you the oasis drink.
Life's strange caravan through the desert winds,
Back toward Nothing; drink—afore the stars sink.

This caravan of life passes mysteriously;
Mayest thou seize the moment that passes happily
Cup-bearer, why grieve about the sorrow of thy patrons
Bring forth the wine-cup, for the night wanes.

O unenlightened race of humankind,
Ye are a nothing, built on empty wind!
Yea, a mere nothing, hovering in the abyss,
A void before you, and a void behind!

Life's hardships are oft softened by beauty,
Its weaknesses oft strengthened by the truth:
Such when roses blossom as realizations
Beauty itself blooms from the well of truth.

— The Persian Life and Temperament —

The Patience Stone is the most empathetic
Of listeners, absorbing into it
The pains and sorrows of the one telling.
When it's full of ache, it bursts into bits.

Persian life simplifies to the extremes,
Loving or fierce, to have or not the means,
Twin Genii granting the best and the worst—
Beyond the Sultan's favor and Fate's gleams.

The subsistence aplenty engendered
By the sun's bounty and breezes rendered
Contrasts to the simoom, the plague, the wars,
The mirage, and the beasts endangered.

Life or death hangs by a skin of water—
In a realm so large to die no better
From a freeze in the north to suffocate
From the heat in the south, weather-whether.

Temper's all poetry and religion,
And there are but two days distinction—

The Day of the Lot—origination,
And the Day of Judgement—destination.

A-tween, inexorable Destiny
Weaves life's braided wave, warp, and woof, Sufi,
Whose virtue is courage and submission
To what has been appointed so surely.

Exquisitely pleasured by poetry,
The senses excite beyond rein, dearly,
Through verses chanted, that drive the fearless—
Then grant reward, returned from victory.

Verse exhilaration bests the grapevine,
For quatrains and couplets exceed fine wine.
Flowers and tenders are as drink-spirits,
With the rose gleam a dram of hashish shine.

The Persian pearls bear the down of the lip,
The mole on the cheek, the eyelash, tulips,
Lilies, roses, jasmines, pearls, musk, birds, song—
Epigrammatic, and often epic.

Poetry dresses the phantasmic new
By enshrining life's apparitional brew,
Captured and bottled as aqua-vita—
Wisdom's pearls, from the evanescent dew.

The cedar, the cypress, the palm, the olive,
The willow, and fig-tree, and birds therein,
Are ne'er wanting in the musky verses,
Nor the flower legends, as well as wind.

What's pent and smouldered as the numb and dumb
Is not spent in the poet, but from a crumb
Rises and grows over into new form,
As relief, in creation through his plumb.

Of a keen bodily sense with sensation,
With a deep intellectual passion,
Poets wing far between Heaven and Earth—
As delight in the two's composition.

A snatch of poem the camel-driver sings,
And paints with sun-beams what his vision brings—
Of the waving veils adorning the tent,
Of the pipe-dreams floating up in smoke rings...

Which fumes are as sighs sent to Heaven far,
For consideration, from his altar
On this bubbled puff of a worldly sphere,
In case Destiny wishes to shake its jar.

The fence is a temptation for a flout,
Yet souls are the breezes that have no route.
Were that I was her soft breath in and out,
I could e'er on my way kiss her lips' pout.

In the night of your tresses, the day flees;
In the round of your rose lips, naught but these;
In your walking, waking form, on my knees;
Of your swelling breasts, oh, please to show, please.

Coffee plants are in the desert first seen,
By a starving outcast, who eats the bean,
And finds it bitter, so he boils some, tart,
Finding that the water is the better part.

Such from asylum he returns home, quaint,
And for his coffee is declared a saint,
But its drinkers are despised by clerics—
The partakers dally over their cups!

THE FALSE AND THE TRUE

51.
Would you that spangle of Existence spend
About The Secret—quick about it, Friend!
A Hair perhaps divides the False from True—
And upon what, prithee, may life depend?

52.
A Hair perhaps divides the False and True;
Yes; and a single Alif were the clue—
Could you but find it—to the Treasure-house,
And peradventure to The Master too;

Forget about the blame and also the fame—
The Great Wheel's not designed in any name,
Since, with no beginning, it ne'er became;
Thus no Alif through Ye: it's e'er the same.

My spirit to the causeless was near blind:
Quoth I, 'If the Beginning you could find—
The Alif—of word, phrase, and uni-verse,
Thou needs not the alphabet—all's been mined.'

How wondrous this! How mysterious that!
There's nowhere else to look for life's impact;
We must experience the wonder and
Mystery of life in every single act.

Seize the moment or lose its momentum,
Wearing time as your royal diadem;
Richly accelerate life's momentous gem,
Letting your motto be 'Carpe diem'.

World does not pass by; you pass through it;
Clear your being so the treasure may arrive;
This spirit sparkles of a different light,
The gemstones are of a different mine.

53.

Whose secret Presence through Creation's veins
Running Quicksilver-like eludes your pains;
Taking all shapes from Máh to Máhi and
They change and perish all—but He remains;

'Tis best all other blessings to forego
For wine, that charming Turki maids bestow;
Kalendars' raptures pass all things that are,
From moon on high down into fish below!

The best of all that is above the moon
And below the fish is beauty's commune,
In her wine poured and sipped, all else forgone,
From Mah to Mahi, raptured noon to noon.

Oh sweet, almond-eyed fortune of love's glow,
Our life-streams flow toward the great below.
In Fate's clutch, back into dust we must go,
So let us liquify 'long life's plateau.

54.

A moment guessed—then back behind the Fold
Immerst of Darkness round the Drama roll'd
Which, for the Pastime of Eternity,
He doth Himself contrive, enact, behold.

'Twas writ at first, whatever was to be,
By pen, unheeding bliss or misery,
Yea, writ upon the tablet once for all,
To murmur or resist is vanity.

Outputs must have inputs, they in turning
Becoming inputs to more fates churning;
In that sense, all is writ, on every path,
As in ours, so what must be will e'er spring.

THE VAIN PURSUIT

55.
But if in vain, down on the stubborn Floor
Of Earth, and up to Heav'n's unopening Door,
You gaze To-day, while You are You—how then
To-morrow, when You shall be You no more.

56.
Perplext no more with Human or Divine,
To-morrow's tangle to the winds resign,
And lose your fingers in the tresses of
The Cypress-slender Minister of Wine.

Without the bitter there's no balance sweet;
From my height of youth lies the valley deep;
Even the biting grape loses its tartness;
'Tis not the wine that changes, but's my own feat.

57.
Waste not your Hour, nor in the vain Pursuit
Of This and That endeavour and Dispute?
Better be merry with the fruitful Grape
Than sadden after none, or bitter, Fruit.

I don't know if what made me doth appoint
To Joy or Pain when this world I disjoint,
Or whether, but I do know life and verse;
Hence with love and wine I myself anoint.

THE DIVORCE OF REASON

58.
You know, my Friends, how long since in my House
For a new Marriage I did make Carouse:
Divorced old barren Reason from my Bed,
And took the Daughter of the Vine to Spouse.

My heart's blood gleams like a melted ruby,
The wealth of mine—the gem that flows in me;
My goblet enshrines my wounded heart's tears—
Wine is my soul and the cup my body.

Rubies from the vine's mines are melted up,
As the moon-veil dissolved in the sun's sup,
In pearled crystal goblets of the flow;
Oh, sparkle with life's essence sweet—thy cup!

As clouds' down to jasmine blossoms doth shred,
From violet unto the green garden bed,
Out of the bluish-purple grape, I pour
Into my lily-cup the wine bled so red.

59.

For "Is" and "Is-Not" though with Rule and Line,
And "Up-And-Down" by logic I define,
Of all that one should care to fathom, I
Was never deep in anything but—Wine.

Parch not thy self with old arguments' heat,
O'er 'is' or 'is not' of some hidden street,
But drench thyself with the juicy grape,
Lest you sour, leaving dry raisins to eat.

With brows and beard I brush the tavern door,
And drop the worlds good and ill on the floor.
If they should bounce and roll to my own street,
I would quick kick them along all the more.

If some say of ways to make things from naught,
They're right back to the 'IS' eterne, ne'er wrought,
For 'ways' are something: capability;
'IS' has no choice—it must be, and ne'er not.

60.

Ah, but my computations, People say,
Have squared the Year to human Compass, eh?

**If so, by striking from the Calendar
Unborn To-morrow and dead Yesterday.**

**There are two days about which we needn't ask,
The one that hasn't come and the one that's past,
For we live in the paradisal 'now',
In which each moment is eternally vast!**

*The unborn future is inherent in the past,
Its 'will be' is real, with no unreal contrast class,
As there's no opposite to existence—no Nil;
It's not just that future is going to exist.*

*The moment contains eternal reward;
Both past and future are rolled thereinward.
Time never passes; it stays as it is;
Still, it is ceaselessly moving onward.*

*March, April! Spring! We'll reign as we May there,
Between June and her sister September,
Then prolong the Fall, till November come
December, when we can sweet Remember.*

*Take the road of 'Eventually' toward 'Someday';
Turn back at the fork of 'Maybe' and 'Perhaps';
Pass the winding path where 'It Could Have Been';
Then you've arrived in the land of 'Never'!*

THE JARRING SECTS

61.

**And lately, by the Tavern Door agape,
Came stealing through the Dusk an Angel Shape,
Bearing a vessel on his Shoulder; and
He bid me taste of it; and 'twas—the Grape!**

62.

The Grape that can with Logic absolute
The Two-and-Seventy jarring Sects confute:
The subtle Alchemist that in a Trice
Life's leaden Metal into Gold transmute.

Let the two-and-seventy sects, all told,
Diverge in their tales of myth-takes so old;
One draught of alkimiya wine cures all ills,
Transforming life's leaden dross into gold.

Athirst, I quench and drench in wine's romance,
Which troubles not Heaven's glance, perchance.
Did the All-Seeing's thoughts not grant the chance?
Then God's All-Knowing is but ignorance.

If wine they forbid, then naught for whose sake,
And of no companions life's ills to shake,
Nor the genial company prolonged;
Seems those who drink are of reason wide awake.

63.

The mighty Mahmud, the victorious Lord,
That all the misbelieving and black Horde
Of Fears and Sorrows that infest the Soul
Scatters and slays with his enchanted Sword.

Ghuz tribes had looted Naishapur
And burned it to the ground several times,
And it had been the scene of bloody wars
Between the Seljuqs and Ghaznavids dynasties.

The world turns, shadows fly, energy spreads apace,
Consolidating here and there, not an impatient race.
Muslims crash the gates, and now New Rome is cleft,
A prism of many-splendored light is all that's left.

THE VINE

64.

Why, be this Juice the growth of God, who dare
Blaspheme the twisted tendril as a Snare?
A Blessing, we should use it, should we not?
And if a Curse—why, then, Who set it there?

Why call wicked the nectar of the vine?
What bane is it to cure the heart with wine?
Bad water? Phish, 'tis Heaven's good water.
Bring out the physic for this life of mine.

As thin as air, wine is spirit's rare gift,
An ethereal sprite whose flow is swift.
Heavy-wits aren't fit to leaden my float,
But heavy wine casks are so light to lift.

Many a snare Thou placed into life's way,
And into our nature temptation's sway,
Of Your entrapment, not all are aware.
'Tis not our debt; Thou should all the price pay.

65.

I must abjure the Balm of Life, I must,
Scared by some After-reckoning ta'en on trust,
Or lured with Hope of some Diviner Drink,
To fill the Cup—when crumbled into Dust!

Whether where, 'twixt raw Divine and ripe wine?
Which the lure enshrine; which the snare intwine?
In taverns, incline, wise with love, than decline,
As dumb in the monastery confine.

The deceptive who make belief a law,
A distinction 'tween soul and body draw,
Yet, on my split hairs I'll place a wine jug,
E'en if they'd put a cock's comb after all.

66.

If but the Vine and Love-abjuring Band
Are in the Prophet's Paradise to stand,
Alack, I doubt the Prophet's Paradise
Were empty as the hollow of one's Hand.

Why would the All Knowing, Loving Expert
Compose with Power His designed concert,
Then decompose His meant Magnificat?
Because there's none Such beyond the turret.

The Voices of the Past

67.

If I myself upon a looser Creed
Have loosely strung the Jewel of Good Deed,
Let this one thing for my Atonement plead:
That One for Two I never did misread.

68.

Strange, is it not? that of the myriads who
Before us pass'd the door of Darkness through,
Not one returns to tell us of the Road,
Which to discover we must travel too.

69.

The Revelations of Devout and Learn'd
Who rose before us, and as Prophets burn'd,
Are all but Stories, which, awoke from Sleep
They told their comrades, and to Sleep return'd.

Saki, they who so discussed and fussed,
Have long since bow'd their sleepy heads to crust;
Go thou fetch wine, but hear the truth from me,
Their lore be wind, their lofty themes are dust.

Some quaff wine, deep, as the late hours creep
And some all night in their mosque-vigil weep.

All drift around the sea, blind to the shore;
Only One's awake, while all others sleep.

THE SOUL'S ANSWER

70.
Why, if the Soul can fling the Dust aside,
And naked on the Air of Heaven ride,
Were't not a Shame—were't not a Shame for him
In this clay carcass crippled to abide?

If spirit, freed from mortal coil, could soar
Back through cold, empty space to Heaven's door,
Its native home lies far beyond the sky,
And shame it was to bear this foreign shore.

71.
'Tis but a Tent where takes his one day's rest
A Sultan to the realm of Death addrest;
The Sultan rises, and the dark Ferrash
Strikes, and prepares it for another Guest.

Yon Heaven's Wheel flings its comet portent,
The plot to end our lives unimportant.
To the lawn, love, for one day we shall be
As the grass that grows about our tent.

72.
I sent my Soul through the Invisible,
Some letter of that After-life to spell:
And by and by my Soul return'd to me,
And answer'd "I Myself am Heav'n and Hell:"

The sky, a vault, spans our worn lives below;
Jihun a course from our strained eyes aflow;
Hell is a spark struck by our vain distress;
Heaven but an instant when content we know.

Pen, tablet, Heaven and Hell I looked to see
Above the skies, from all Eternity;
At last the Master Sage instructed me,
"Pen, tablet, Heaven and Hell are all in thee."

The world is but a belt of fading years,
The Oxus but the trace of running tears,
And Hell is but the spark of futile toil,
And Paradise a flash of fleeting cheers.

I fear not death, Heaven, or even Hell,
For death is only life's natural knell,
And Heaven and Hell are within myself;
The one thing I fear is not living well!

73.
Heav'n but the Vision of fulfill'd Desire,
And Hell the Shadow from a Soul on fire,
Cast on the Darkness into which Ourselves,
So late emerged from, shall so soon expire.

Oh heart, here the Fount of Truth does not rain,
Nor do we from subtle sages gain.
'Tis here that with a loving heart Heav'n's made,
For thou may'st ne'er another Heaven attain.

Wooing the fair ones and draining the cup,
Beats by far the fanatic's zealous yup.
If drunkards and lovers are doomed to Hell,
Then none will e'er of Heaven take a sup.

"Where in the Woe is Purgatory's bane?"
Purgatory's on Venus, where sulfurs rain.
"Where in the Heck is that deep Hell of pain?"
Hell's found in the sun's heart, oh hot burning pain!

"Where in the name of Heaven is Paradisea?"
Of Heaven's site no one has any idea—

"*Really now, where's Heaven, one and the same?*"
It's the world's best kept secret: Earth is its name!

"*Yes, that's said, but truly, where is the stead...*"
I must tell of them that they're only read;
"*...Of those places spent after we are dead?*"
It's written of words that language bred.

"'*Twas hope-word that invented All that was said?*"
'*Twas these that were signed for anything Divine 'said'.*

From Heaven's stars spewed the dust eterne;
Time's seas nurtured thee and thine in turn.
From time, death, and dust we thus became,
And by this, thus, and that we must return.

Time and stardust made us Earth's living guest,
When quick death sifted the rest from the best.
Those three, our birthright, write our epitaph:
RIP; time expires, death comes, dust is left.

We are life's eternal creative smile,
Beaming as the universal epistyle.
In us the Cosmos has come alive;
Such we borrow life from death for awhile.

Earth couldn't be farther out in space, alone;
In all directions it rolls along, unknown.
Look to yon stars piercing the depths of time:
They beckon, warm and welcome, the fires of home.

Among the lights that dance in the sky,
A haven waits in sight for you and I,
A world where flowers bloom and fountains spray,
A paradise called Earth to glorify.

Earth's a garden, an oasis in space,
A planet of boundless beauty and grace.

One might search the heavens for such in vain,
Finding no equal, any time or place.

THE FATES PLAYING GAMES

74.
But leave the Wise to wrangle, and with me
The Quarrel of the Universe let be:
And, in some corner of the Hubbub couch'd,
Make Game of that which makes as much of Thee.

I'll play the game and roll the Earthly dies,
And through this worldly life enjoy the prize;
If Earth is Hell for love's adventurers,
Then I wish no more for God's Paradise.

"What the meaning to this play we're befit,
From dirt to dust within the script that's writ?"
The wise in search have thrown themselves to waste;
Experience alone is the benefit.

75.
For in and out, above, about, below,
'Tis nothing but a Magic Shadow-show,
Play'd in a Box whose Candle is the Sun,
Round which we Phantom Figures come and go.

We are phenomena's projected face,
Well-painted from noumena's unseen base;
It's as a lamp lights up a paper shade,
We figures revolving around in space.

Our being blocks the view of the Ultimate,
Nor to gaze at it can we our selves acquit.
Ev'n the wise can't step beyond their nature—
All mothers' sons stand helpless before it.

We are magic lanterns shining here;
Our spirits are the lights in there.
From what bright star came the gleam in your eyes?
From what distant sun came your smile, light-wise?

Come, light your lantern and mine with good cheer;
We're magic lamps; our spirits dance in here.
Our beginnings and ends are of nowhere,
So, let's radiate, since for now we're here!

Our minds and senses interpret and dispense
The base reality into the colors and sensations
Of the phenomenal world from the noumenal;
We may become either rainbows or ugly stains!

Mind, like Shelley's prism of many-colored glass,
Strains the white radiance of Eternity
Into our being—until death tramples us—
And then back we must go—to stardust.

NIGHTS AND DAYS

76.

'Tis all a Chequer-board of Nights and Days
Where Destiny with Men for Pieces plays:
Hither and thither moves, and mates, and slays,
And one by one back in the Closet lays.

The wings of time are checkered black and white,
As fluttering round the day flies the night.
As chess pieces, we gamely play for life,
Until into the box we return, quite!

Oh, Idol, whose cheeks reflect on the rose,
The King of Babylon as much as you knows.
He moves castles, pawns, knights, bishops, and queens,
Of You His glance and Yours back, through the rows.

midnight

Oh, Shah, you were throned through Destiny Old,
The steeds of empire saddled as your fold,
And where thy charger plants its gilded hooves,
On some dusty clay, the earth turns to gold.

One wing is black and the other is white,
As the bird flies overhead and around—
Life's checkerboard pattern, we've found,
Forms most magically all over the ground.

He Knows

77.

The Ball no Question makes of Ayes and Noes,
But Right or Left as strikes the Player goes;
And He that toss'd Thee down into the Field,
He knows about it all—HE knows—HE knows!

Rigged and jigged, God's perfect plans would be done,
But he'd long for some surprises yet to come,
So, He might even roll the dice, it being 'random';
'Damn!' He'd say, 'I already know the outcome!'

The Diviner would just sit around, naught to do,
His mind already full with what would become new.
He couldn't play dice, scrambling the forecast,
For He would know all of which the die was cast.

Rejoice, for your goose was cooked long ago,
Your future eggs laid 'fore you were aglow.
Ne'er can be recalled the bird that has flown,
So love life's flight, on the winds that must blow.

Fate's Wheel soft whispers in my ear, 'I know
What's been decreed—just ask and I will show.'
Were mine the hand that made myself revolve,
I should have saved myself from reeling so.

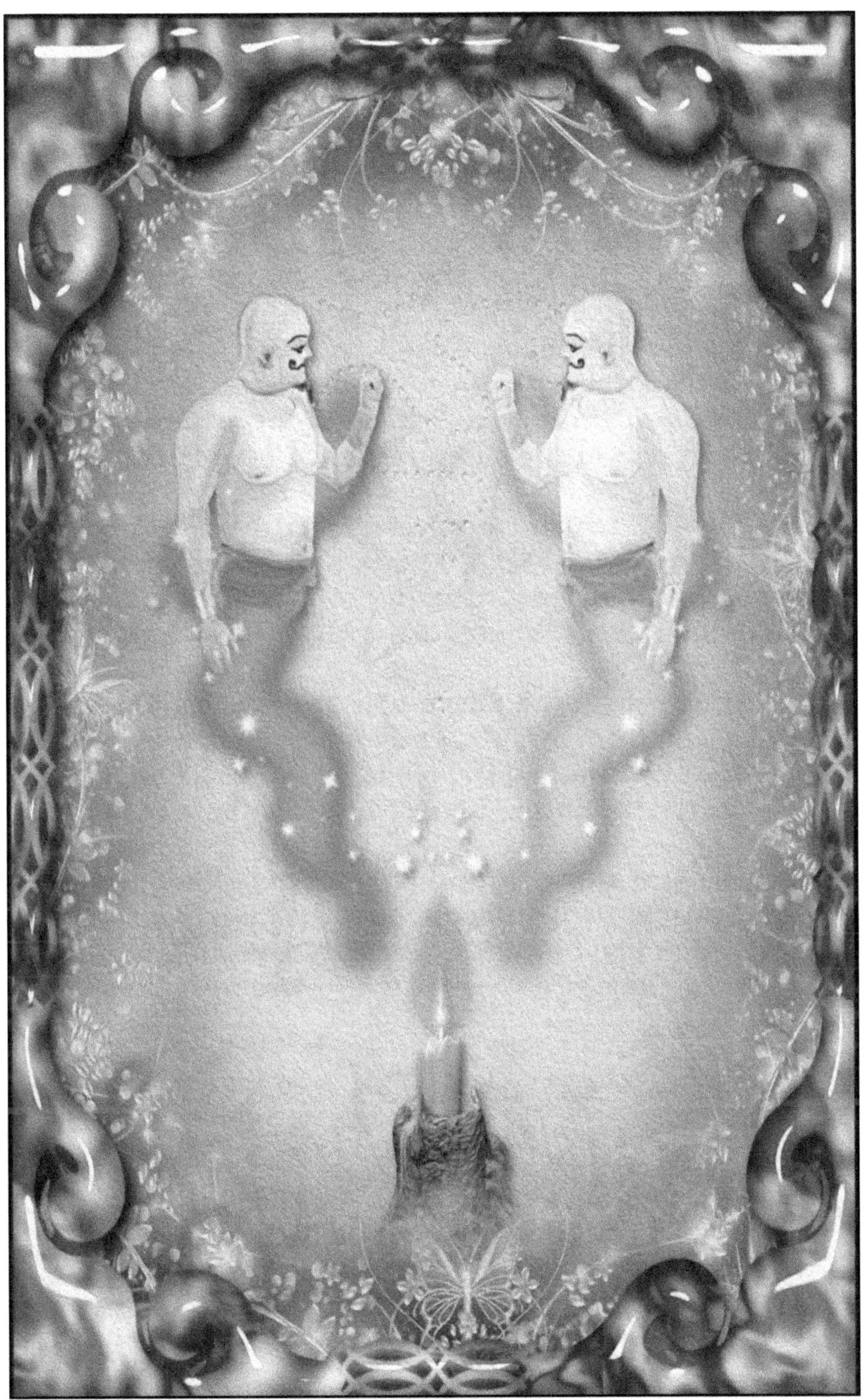

THE MOVING FINGER

78.

The Moving Finger writes; and, having writ,
Moves on: nor all thy Piety nor Wit
Shall lure it back to cancel half a Line,
Nor all thy Tears wash out a Word of it.

Now's pen inscribes, based on what was there,
Its destined words phrasing our sentence here.
Although it may spell to us right or wrong,
Even one letter's change hasn't a prayer.

What be: thy output must form from input,
For naught else can stride the moving foot,
And 'randoms' recede; naught from nought makes no.
The pen can't revise its scroll; 'we're' caput!

Relate my good deeds o'er and o'er again,
And forgive each fault, sin, and crime times ten.
Let's not kindle, stir, blow, or fan the flame;
Grace is Divine; no need to ink the pen.

As to the rich and variegated sheet
Of plumage of the peacock, all hearts beat
And quick cry out with its splendourous spread.
Would that bird then blush for its ugly feet?

LIMITATIONS

79.

O Thou who burn'st in Heart for those who burn
In Hell, whose fires thyself shall feed in turn,
How long be crying, 'Mercy on them, God!'
Why, who art Thou to teach, and He to learn?

The unlocked Secret gleams in the tavern,
But in the mosque the key remains unturned.
Oh Thou Planner, Designer, and Mixer,
I'm Thy own recipe to love or burn.

Though we can ne'er know the Ultimate named,
From that fact something profound is still framed;
It's that when one can't know, one must still live,
And as such in that life cannot be blamed.

Oh you with "Special Creation's" conceit,
Thy pride judges the soused mystics you meet.
Bring not awake the vipers from their sleep;
For peace, hail those humble souls of the street.

Their lives are their own, not yours for distain;
If thou desires three worlds' peace, then refrain
From smothering the kisses of their bliss,
Lest you agitate your own flame in vain.

The man-writ Koran is nought but a mime,
Lying unread, sprouting dust; but, through wine,
Read from the cup mouth's etched rim, the glowing
Words flow, in converse, from its lip to mine.

On and on they say of Who paved the way,
Then even tell the nature of such Theity,
And on and on they presume further upon,
Joining that group called 'On and On Anon'.

Our blind-fated path was the further paved
When disasters finished most of the species.
Far from a feature of Intelligent Design,
It opened up the space that was needed.

80.
For let Philosopher and Doctor preach
Of what they will, and what they will not—each

Is but one Link in an eternal Chain
That none can slip, nor break, nor over-reach.

"Since outputs always have inputs, so true,
Then what, we wonder, should we try to do?"
It's the other way around, oh, brain stew,
For cause, time, and the universe do you!

The chain is forged that links a thousand deaths
To a thousand future-generated breaths
When lips ripe as fruit gently part in pain:
The smile of a corpse is life touched by death.

81.
And that inverted Bowl we call The Sky,
Whereunder crawling coop't we live and die,
Lift not thy hands to It for help—for It
Rolls impotently on as Thou or I.

The weight of the world I bear on my back;
'Tis mine to own, so there's nought that I lack.
I've everything, and a place to put it;
After it crushes me to dust, I'll unpack.

The bowl of life will drain you from your soul,
Hence thou wilt pull the veil or be as coal;
So you might as well drink the wine of life;
One knows not what's writ, or if, on the scroll.

The overturned bowl as Heaven's dome traps
Those thereunder born crawling toward collapse.
Note the friendship of the bottle and cup:
Blood flows lip to lip, as might yours, perhaps.

What 'IS' can no more not exist than it
Can rule any of what goes on in it;
Impute not thy blame, shame, or fame to it—
Fate's Wheel's more helpless than all within it.
Look at the stars in the depths of the night;

Hold their flames in your mind, keeping them bright.
Their power flows, energizing you, from
The Eternal Charger—you see the light!

Soul to soul, the rays reveal: 'I'm the light,
Thy spirit's sight, a beauty bold and bright,
An inspiration come from darkest night,
A newborn star aglow with insight.'

A thousand starry goblets fill the sky,
So we can taste Heaven's drink when we die.
This is only man's tale, so drink today;
The stars shine on, heedless of where we lie.

Drain thy goblet's nectar of the moon's shine,
While your light sparkles in this 'now' of thine;
Reign with Night's Queen
and drink deep the King's wine,
For the morrow may not find you in time.

THE LAST MAN

82.

With Earth's first Clay They did the Last Man's knead,
And then of the Last Harvest sow'd the Seed:
Yea, the first Morning of Creation wrote
What the Last Dawn of Reckoning shall read.

I don't much mind what Idol they adore,
Nor what structures all the more they implore;
But, when they state it all as truth and fact,
This misleads, at best, and's dishonest more!

83.

Yesterday This Day's Madness did prepare;
To-Morrow's Silence, Triumph, or Despair:

Drink! for you not know whence you came, nor why:
Drink! for you know not why you go, nor where.

OMAR'S HOROSCOPE

84.
I tell Thee this—When, starting from the Goal,
Over the shoulders of the flaming Foal
Of Heav'n Parwin and Mushtari they flung,
In my predestin'd Plot of Dust and Soul.

In heaven is seen the bull we name Parwin,
Beneath the earth another lurks unseen;
And thus to wisdom's eyes mankind appear
A drove of asses, two great bulls between!

When Allah set the course of the sun,
And pro-creed the Pleiades their place to run,
Our lot too was fixed in fate's high court;
So why blame us for wrongs that fate has done?

The lodgers of the graves to dust decay,
Ignorant of self, and soon outside are they,
Their unleashed atoms floating through the air,
As mirages, until the judgment-day.

We sleep the sleep that only lovers know,
As front to back, under the blankets' throw,
While meteors criss-cross the darkling skies—
Our floating selves through love and wine aglow.

Near dawn, she stirs the glowing embers of
The watch-fire, and whispers softly, with love,
It's as a transparent veil has lifted;
The stars have gone and the dome shines above.

Colored stars pierce the veil of formless night,
Gemming Heaven's gloried, crown-jeweled might;

In the depths of the deep we live, anon:
We're all alone here to weather the plight.

Omar, the moon's ring binds us truly here,
Wherein from the strict world we disappear—
They to wonder hence whither whence we went:
Love, kisses, and selves bonded to endear.

85.

The Vine had struck a Fibre; which about
It clings my Being—let the Sufi flout;
Of my Base Metal may be filed a Key,
That shall unlock the Door he howls without.

86.

And this I know: whether the one True Light,
Kindle to Love, or Wrath consume me quite,
One Glimpse of It within the Tavern caught
Better than in the Temple lost outright.

The wine-jar is our sacred place of prayer—
We drink in lessons of true being here
Let's pass much more time in taverns, so that
Our time misspent in mosques we can repair.

"I'm the darkest," boasts the Shadow to the Night.
"No," gloats Midnight, "compared to me you're bright."
"You floodlights!" crows Starless Space,
"Stop your fight.
The darkest plight is the lack of Love's delight!"

Good and Evil sprang from Wrong and Right,
When from naught twin Genii split day and night.
Oh, fear not that black's might can vanquish white;
Darkest night can't e'en quench the smallest light!

We dare to walk the line, balancing fun
There, between adventure and misfortune,

For the greatest blunder in life is to
Repeatedly fear that we might make one.

The stars are not just white, they scintillate:
Sirius is blue, its companion green;
Betelgeuse, red; many, like Sol, yellow;
Arcturus, orange—all jewels constellate.

I played a fine trick on the Shah last night;
I said that I'd bring down the star light
Of his favorite sky pattern to ground;
My sparklers dug into the sand lit bright!

ENTRAPMENT

87.
What! out of senseless Nothing to provoke
A conscious Something to resent the yoke
Of unpermitted Pleasure, under pain
Of Everlasting Penalties, if broke!

He binds us in resistless Nature's chain,
And yet bids us our natures to restrain;
Between these counter rules we stand perplexed:
Hold the jar slant, but all the wine retain.

O turn away those roguish eyes of thine!
Be still! seek not my peace to undermine!
Thou say'st, "Look not." "I might as well essay
To slant my goblet, and not spill my wine.

We lay in the cloak of Naught, asleep and still,
Thou said'st, "Awake! taste the world's good and ill;"
Here we are puzzled by Thy strange command,
From slanted jars no single drop to spill.

Khayyam, why fret o'er spilling drops of sin
From life's temptation glass filled to the brim?
Play with that imaginary friend: Him;
What is mercy for but to save thy skin!

Ne'er I've strung Thy rosarium deeds pearled,
Nor swabbed sin's dusty beads soiling my world;
Yet, I'm not hopeless of Thy pardon's grace,
For I have judged that Two is One unfurled.

My nature is what it is, not tame,
As intended, making me not to blame,
Though some this don't know, and throw pain & shame,
So let's claim mercy, too, and clear my name.

The Cup-Bearer's Self, too, flows to the brim
And, like us, can't help but spill o'er the rim,
Which grape-juiced droplets extinguish fired eyes;
Praise Allah; we've the balm for life's pangs grim.

Life's cruelty satisfies all repentance,
So this credit give me when Thy sentence,
While here, too, I sin to cancel Your debt,
And away from the holy mosque jump the fence.

During the short Earthly shrift time is swift,
So in love and wine there's no need for thrift;
They prate, "May God to thee grant penitence."
He gives it not, nor would I take the gift.

Such as I am, Thy power created me,
Thy care hath kept me for a century!
Through all these years I make experiment,
If my sins or Thy mercy greater be.

The light of Heav'n did the Earth illumine,
When He shaped human nature's acumen.
Temptations He then placed everywhere,
But He'll punish us for being human!

Who's the scribe; what slab is written upon?
Where's horrid Hell, and gloried Heaven yon?
I asked Myself of such stylus and slate:
'You're both the dancer and the danced upon'.

88.
What! from his helpless Creature be repaid
Pure Gold for what he lent us dross-allay'd—
Sue for a Debt we never did contract,
And cannot answer—Oh the sorry trade!

89.
Nay, but, for terror of his wrathful Face,
I swear I will not call Injustice Grace;
Not one Good Fellow of the Tavern but
Would kick so poor a Coward from the place.

Of dust and dirt, throw the more on His face,
And fling prayer, praise, and rites for fair embrace;
Quaff the cup; what time for faith's endeavor?
None have returned here from any Place.

Heed not Sunna Law, nor so-called Divine,
Yet to the poor your last morsel assign,
Afflict not, nor slander, and give love to all;
Of these I warrant thee future—bring wine!

Send into the graveyard the Five Hour Prayer,
And off to the tavern to live life's dare;
When we gaze on a long-necked flask of wine,
We'll stretch our necks in kind that wine to share.

Lay waste to the rites of prayer and fasting;
Shatter faith's pious claims neverlasting;
Slam fast the gate on myth-spells arriving.
Drink, and be kind to all of life's casting.

Drink wine; 'tis the life saver on storm's sea;
Let the sorrows drown in a continued spree;

We have friends, love, books, and flowers to share:
Parentheses within eternity!

Give me wine as balm to soothe the heart's lull,
The salve, the boon that relieves all that's dull;
There's more cheer in a single drop than in
The Vault of Heaven hollow as a skull.

I drink the "foe of faith", they tell so,
Right and left, expurgating, from their 'knows'.
Well, then, by God, as I know, I'll drink more;
It's right that I should drink the blood of foes!

Mosque for me is rare, yet there I repair,
So there I'm a prayer, of feint pious air.
I had stolen a fine prayer-carpet there
That's now worn, so I need one more than fair.

They believe, through fear of Hell's misery,
Lured onward by Heaven's reward to be,
Yet he who lives real, and thus knows what 'IS',
Never fires his heart from chaff's smoke tree.

Draw pure the blood from the throat of the jug,
And stain the tulip-hued wine on your mug.
Where could you find a better friend than wine,
So pure, so snug? Well, not on a prayer rug.

He to whom reason has inscribed its script
Upon his self will revel unto the crypt.
Lest disposing his will to phantasms,
He navigates his heart's ship well equipped.

90.

Oh Thou who didst with Pitfall and with Gin
Beset the Road I was to wander in,
Thou wilt not with Predestination round
Enmesh me, and impute my Fall to Sin?

IN THE BEGINNING

91.

Oh Thou, who Man of baser Earth didst make,
And who with Eden didst devise the Snake;
For all the Sin wherewith the Face of Man
Is blacken'd, Man's Forgiveness give—and take!

With flora mystical and magical,
Eden's botanical garden was blest,
So Eve, taking more than just the Apple,
Plucked off the loveliest of the best.

Thus it's to Eve that we must give our thanks,
For Earth's variety of fruits and plants,
For when she was out of Paradise thrown,
She stole all the flowers we've ever known.

Heaven's patron of arts, grace, and license
Left us sweet-smelling plants with flowered scents
And aromas redolent—florescence
In flush and prime of days reminiscent.

Kuza—Nama.
("Book of Pots")

IN THE POTTER'S HOUSE

92.

Listen again. One Evening at the Close
Of Ramazan, ere the better Moon arose,
In that old Potter's Shop I stood alone
With the clay Population round in Rows.

93.

And once again there gather'd a scarce heard
Whisper among them; as it were, the stirr'd

Ashes of some all but extinguisht Tongue,
Which mine ear kindled into living Word.

THE UNGAINLY POT

94.
Said one among them—"Surely not in vain
My substance from the common Earth was ta'en,
That He who subtly wrought me into Shape
Should stamp me back to common Earth again."

THE DESTROYER

95.
Another said—"Why, ne'er a peevish Boy
Would break the Bowl from which he drank in Joy;
Shall He that made the Vessel in pure Love
And Fansy, in an after Rage destroy!"

96.
None answer'd this; but after Silence spake
A Vessel of a more ungainly Make:
"They sneer at me for leaning all awry;
What? did the Hand then of the Potter shake?"

THE LOQUACIOUS VESSELS

97.
And strange to tell, among that Earthen Lot
Some could articulate, while others not:
And suddenly one more impatient cried—
"Who is the Potter, pray, and who the Pot?"

98.
Said one—"Folks of a surly Tapster tell,
And daub his Visage with the Smoke of Hell;

They talk of some strict Testing of us—Pish!
He's a Good Fellow, and 'twill all be well."

BY-AND-BYE

99.
Then said another with a long-drawn Sigh,
"My Clay with long oblivion is gone dry:
But, fill me with the old familiar Juice,
Methinks I might recover by-and-bye!"

After I'm tread in the stead of the dead,
And rooted up after my blood's drained red,
See to it that naught but a wine jug's made,
For its scent will restore my spirit fled.

THE END OF RAMADAN

100.
So, while the Vessels one by one were speaking,
One spied the little Crescent all were seeking:
And then they jogg'd each other, "Brother! Brother!
Hark to the Porter's Shoulder-knot a-creaking!"

Ramadan's now past, and Shawwál comes back,
So feast, song, and pleasure no more we lack;
Now porters with their loads stand back to back,
"Here comes the camel with his precious pack."

The man of spirit, wine renounces ne'er.
The wine that to Life's water doth compare,
In Ramazan if one needs must abstain,
At least let it be abstinence from prayer.

What matters where, what, when, or even who?
In life's fill, any narrative will do.

Drink in ev'ry phase of the lunar month,
The cup waxing and waning, just like you.

OMAR'S TOMB'S FUMES

101.

Ah, with the Grape my fading Life provide,
And wash my Body whence the life has died,
And in a Windingsheet of Vine-leaf wrapt,
So bury me by some sweet Garden-side.

Whence my mystique has fled, wine-blush my cheek,
Wash my body with a vintage antique,
Wrap me in a grapevine leafed windingsheet,
And frame my coffin of cask planks that'll reek.

102.

That e'en my buried Ashes such a Snare
Of Perfume shall fling up into the Air,
As not a True Believer passing by
But shall be overtaken unaware.

Across Khayyàm's gravestone blows the simoom,
Carrying forth Omar's Persia-fume.
Redressed in the versifier's costume,
It's remade into Victorian perfume.

The fumes of ageless rhymes from ancient times
Waft from the Persian verse, as some chimes
New are mixed with the spirit of the old,
Deftly rendered for Victorian climes.

Omar's Persia fumes caught me unawares,
Unveiling Sufi mysteries of theirs—
Eternal spirits recondened from
Universal wisdom he'd gained somewheres.

Through his Rubàiyàt, I sense enchantment,
Essence distilled by the translator's scent.
Recomposed from Khayyàm's dust and spirit,
Potent elixirs escape interment!

Many follow the advice that you give,
Enjoying this life by being active,
But others are deaf, dumb, and blind to sense;
You can lead 'em to life but you can't make 'em live.

103.
Whither resorting from the vernal Heat
Shall Old Acquaintance Old Acquaintance greet,
Under the Branch that leans above the Wall
To shed his Blossom over head and feet.

SPRING RETURNS

104.
Indeed, the Idols I have loved so long
Have done my Credit in Men's Eye much wrong:
Have drown'd my Honour in a shallow Cup,
And sold my Reputation for a Song.

105.
Indeed, indeed, Repentance oft before
I swore—but was I sober when I swore?
And then and then came Spring, and Rose-in-hand
My thread-bare Penitence a-pieces tore.

I look back on my love of life, now old,
The captivating lure that made me bold;
What e'er vestments of penitence I've sewed
Have shredded—in the names of my loves told.

The rose's sweet scent a thorn-prick's worth, 'tis true;
If wine you drink, a headache 'tis worth, too.

The loved one who delights a thousand souls,
Is worth awaiting, give her all her due.

Wandering along the romantic way,
With an houri who drinks life's woes away,
I realize that the cost of a loveless life,
Nor wine, is much too high a price to pay.

Your scent is ripe and your name means nectar.
Exotically blossoming I find you,
As I buzz my way into your flower,
For I am the bee and you my partner.

The rose is the flower that the bee cruises,
Meeting there the butterfly that love chooses;
I unfold the petals of your blossom,
Then drink the nectar of love's sweet juices.

Your wine, my persona radiata,
Fills my golden chalice. Oh, Sultana,
I'm intoxicated by your love-stream
Flowing freely; oh dear, amorata!

Let actions tell what words can never pass:
Pour thy rose-cheeks into my secret's glass,
And thy mouth onto my fare, beloved;
My contrition's been lost in húr morass.

Men and women can't live in isolation,
For like valleys that give rise to mountains,
One's nature makes necessary the other;
When they're joined in love, there's wholeness again.

It was thus the wee fairy women flashed their
Alabaster feet on the hills of Connemara,
That the Houris were dancing for Omar
On Nature's palace floors of Paradise.

I gaze into her glowing eyes that are
As and of a fathomless, moonlit sea,
While her long hair falls all about me like
Like a net of moonbeams, enrapturing me.

(The Trouble with 'Love')
Only a few words rhyme with love above,
Like the overflown dove, the heartless shove,
And the ill-fitting glove. Alas, love's rhymes
Remain unheard of, or aren't well thought of.

106.
And much as Wine has play'd the Infidel,
And robb'd me of my Robe of Honour—well,
I often wonder what the Vintners buy
One half so precious as the Goods they sell.

Ne'er the gems of Mars, Venus, and the moon
Can rival the jewels of wine drops' boon;
What pearled treasures can the wine-sellers buy
One half so precious as sold in their saloon?

Bring thy ruby mined, in a crystal thrust,
The drink that raises one up from the dust,
For who knows what breezes blow into gales.
This world is but a passing whirlwind's gust.

Like as the skies rain down sweet jessamine,
And sprinkle all the meads with eglantine,
Right so, from out this jug of violet hue,
I pour in lily cups this rosy wine.

'Tis we who to wine's yoke our necks incline,
And risk our lives to gain the smiles of wine;
The henchman grasps the flagon by its throat
And squeezes out the life-blood of the vine.

Reason moons to Passion, with logic cool,
"Quench thy inner fire, lest it burn us, fool."

Blazes Venus, "I know What I feel, not Why;
'Tis better you take heed of me—I Rule!"

Imagination lights the mind to shine,
To cool Venus' reasonless passion,
And warm Mars' martial song with compassion;
Between those two orbits, the Earth is mine.

Youth and Age

107.

Alas, that Spring should vanish with the Rose!
That Youth's sweet-scented Manuscript should close!
The Nightingale that in the Branches sang,
Ah, whence, and whither flown again, who knows!

The child in us is warm, playful, and bold,
But can die, ere we know, leaving us cold.
Now this we know: The day we stop being
Playful is the day we start to get old.

Oh, Sorrow, drink wine from that well eterne;
Though it burn, its vintage your ills will turn.
As aquavita, it clears young and old;
What wiser prescription is there to learn?

I've flips, trips, dips, and slips, coming to grips;
For antidote I prescribe in my eclipse:
Bring the rubied grape and the silk stringed lute—
Music to my ears and wine to my lips.

Now my lovers but in memory remain,
And of old friends I have only a name,
So I reach out to my faithful compeer—
The wine cup e'er within my reach to drain.

Of all that I owned, just my cup remains,
Yet I'm free of earth's soiling toil, the rains,

The airs of haughty breath, and Hellfire—
Enkindled here, through fifth element gains.

Once bred, the ideal of that morn is shorn;
So, it's that the ablution, second born,
Is to rinse one's stain with wine, and not mourn,
Since ne'er can be restored what's worn so torn.

In the morning, Thou graced me with the glow,
And I'd the peace of the Heavenly flow;
Then after noon, scorn's heat, then darkness falls;
What of Thy nature in me changed to 'foe'?

From birth we can look forward to being host
To woe, and then to giving up the ghost.
Happy are they who quickly burn to toast,
And blessed are they who ne'er came to the roast.

One may live to sixty, but not much more,
So thy feet should tread but to tavern's door,
And ere thy hollowed skull become a bowl,
Grasp thy glass, lest it drop unto the floor.

Thou hast dropped my jug, now broken, oh Lord,
And it drains its wine into the greensward,
My bliss shattered from Your bung-stumbling.
O Lord, drink You drunk too much from the gourd?

Creation's smoke burns evermore thy meat,
E'en 'fore one cinders into deeper heat.
Ah, shun what bane you may of the kitchen;
Take no stock in trade; all sweet profits eat.

The winter dawn gleams as white as the snow,
Color-blinding us; seek the ruby's glow,
And bring two logs, making of one a lute,
And the other into the fireplace throw.

Now the Earth is very old, but each spring it
Turns young again when nature reinvents it,
Constructing the Temple of Flora outside,
In desert, field, wetland, woodland, and wayside.

Give to one jasmine-bloomed and fairy-born
Thy heart, and of dear friends passed do not mourn,
But unto her glowing breasts rest thy head;
Cast not to the wind but flow on wine bourn.

Oh my desire, bring thy cup and let's go,
O'er lawns to play where crystal waters flow;
Malicious Heaven these lovely faces
A hundred times as pots and cups will show.

Blooms have eternal life in Heaven's glade—
An ethereal floral wonderland
Of everlasting recollections;
Oh but that mortal life would never fade!

THIS SORRY SCHEME

108.
Would but the Desert of the Fountain yield
One glimpse—if dimly, yet indeed, reveal'd,
Toward which the fainting Traveller might spring,
As springs the trampled herbage of the field!

109.
Oh if the World were but to re-create,
That we might catch ere closed the Book of Fate,
And make The Writer on a fairer leaf
Inscribe our names, or quite obliterate!

110.
Better, oh better, cancel from the Scroll
Of Universe one luckless Human Soul,

Than drop by drop enlarge the Flood that rolls
Hoarser with Anguish as the Ages roll.

111.
Ah, Love! could thou and I with Fate conspire
To grasp this sorry Scheme of Things entire,
Would not we shatter it to bits—and then
Re-mould it nearer to the Heart's Desire!

Beyond the pale, aft the last perfect day,
The Earth's atmosphere incinerates away,
Mercury and Venus now within the sun,
For the Crimson Giant is on its way.

Hellholes hurl infernal light-year jets of fear,
In Centaurus, cross the galactic sphere.
Supermassive darkling beasts devour all;
Abandon hope all ye who enter here.

Obliterated by a war nuclear,
The Earth explodes in blazes solar!
Says a child in a galaxy afar,
'Oh, look! Look at the pretty shooting star!'

IN MEMORIAM

112.
Ah, Moon of my Delight who know'st no wane,
The Moon of Heav'n is rising once again:
How oft hereafter rising shall she look
Through this same Garden after me—in vain!

— The Worldly Love Story of the Earth and the Moon —

(Notation: In this section of all Austin's quatrains,
Inspired by Shelley, the moon's voice is in italics font
and the Earth's voice is in regular font.)

I give no reason for love's passion planned,
Since to do so would be but secondhand,
For the Heart and Soul have many reasons
That Reason can never understand.

I am thy moon, thy constant satellite,
Thy crystal paramour of day and night.
Above and below, and within thy sight,
I whirl around you in loving delight.

In a gravnetic dance, I whirl and twirl,
Attracted to you, the liveliest world;
Around you as a necklace I'm aswirl—
Wear me as thy crystalline gem impearled.

Wherever thou orbits 'round Apollo,
I must twirl and whirl, hurry and follow;
Dust I gather, meteors I swallow,
Ranging far and wide through space not hollow.

Thy romantic beam, as Cupid's arrow,
Pierces my heart and kills my sorrow,
Injecting life and love for tomorrow;
Henceforth, I'll shine with this life I borrow.

Around you I whirl, a necklace of pearl,
Trailing afterimages of my world,
Adorning you, thy bosom bountiful,
With crystalline gems of another world.

Oh, moon, thy Earth would wobble like a top
With your steadying influence not,
In turns quick of searing and freezing ruins,
Unto dying soon, without you, oh moon!

As twin planets, our orbits must convolve;
Into each our tidal motions dissolve.
Around a common center we revolve—
The focus from which our passions evolve.

As twin planets, each other's way we pave,
With the push-pulse of the graviton wave.
We're captured, but not as each other's slave,
For to the sun our orbits are concave.

To your lines of flux my path I align—
I'm your constant paramour, crystalline;
Your world pours life on mine, on mine!
Dearest Earth, I must be thine, must be thine!

A magnetic beam emanates from thee,
Attracting me, holding me, kissing me;
Tidal love washes freely over me,
Linking you and me for eternity.

Basking warmly in your reflected light,
I'm bright, oh, so radiant in your sight!
In the love and light of your spirit bright
I need not ever face the endless night.

Your vibrations travel without a sound,
Circling from all directions to surround;
This affection touches me 'round and 'round
And closely binds me to you—I'm love-bound!

We're as different as midnight and noon,
Yet drawn close by the force of Earth and moon;
As lovers we merge in a sweet eclipse,
When world meets world as a kiss on our lips.

Oh, as your shadow of love covers me
I am full, so full in the shade of thee;
When we overlap, that union is us;
The you is in me, the me is in thee!

As moon and Earth, we bathe in radiance,
Cleansing our hearts in love's grand alliance;
Around and around each other we dance,
Entranced by the whirl of our dalliance.

My blood runs warm with the sun's heat at noon.
My spirit is swept by thee, swelling moon.
Space surrounds us. The tides flow through us.
Global rhythms are always playing our tune.

The Earth would wobble like a dying top very soon,
Without the steadying influence of our lovely moon;
But, it's slipping from our grasp
an inch and a half a year.
The end's not so near, but we'll need a way out of here.

113.

Be of Good Cheer—the sullen Month will die,
And a young Moon requite us by and by:
Look how the Old one meagre, bent, and wan
With Age and Fast, is fainting from the Sky!

Oh, thou, beloved, moon of my heart's delight,
I'll bear forth, with new rhymes, from the night,
To unlock, with philosophic logic,
The Secret of Existence and man's plight.

Summer passed away in his sleep last night,
Autumn, sweet and plump, carries his offspring.
The year dies in the night, ghostly winter looms—
Yet spring's flower is already in the seed.

Life is a flower whose leaf is summer green,
Whose spring was purple passion Eglantine.
Although fall's second spring may intervene,
The frost at last is the winter seen.

Not all poems are pleasant—some speak of death,
Of life's end, separate by just a breath;
We see tombstones overgrown, under swept,
Names unknown, and to all the message saith:

'Read Me,' it says, in words engraved beyond the brink,
You who live, up above: of life go drink;

There are those ecstatic moments in which
Nature seems just on the tremulous verge
Of sending to us her magic answer—
During moments of intense reverie.

And you, underneath, now lying so dead:
Rest in peace, relax; it's later than you think!'

The Angel of Light finds Omar to bless,
And says, 'Khayyàm, I must soon repossess
Your clay, so let us drink to your success!'
He drinks and smiles, then meets Life's last caress.

As Omar reclines on the grass, near death.
The Dark Angel arrives and to him saith,
'Drink one last deep drought from Life's precious cup.'
Omar smiles and sips, then breathes his last breath.

114.
Khayyam, who stitched the tents of science,
Has fallen in grief's furnace and been suddenly burned,
The shears of Fate have cut the tent ropes of his life,
And the broker of Hope has sold him for nothing!

Fate Lachesis threaded Khayyam's life long,
So Omar stitched his tent's reasoning strong,
Clotho e'er spinning his essence along;
Atropos then sheared his rope for a song.

The Bird of Time is off and whither flown,
And rides on breezes wherever blown,
Lightly here, slightly there, but after gone,
Leaves the cold vacuum of what once was known.

115.
And when Thyself with shining Foot shall pass
Among the Guests Star-scatter'd on The Grass,
And in Thy joyous Errand reach the Spot
Where I made one—turn down an empty Glass!

Then, unto love's moonlight tryst, arm in arm,
Aft taking delight in each others charm,
Raise thy glasses once more in blessing, and
Cheer the one who lived and died without alarm.

The impossible dream we'd of our fate
Was to outwit life's expiration date,
To be deathless and somehow carry on;
We'll live, anon, in the lives we've touched, mate!

Sad Yesterday, Today, and Tomorrow,
They all come, led by their tears and sorrow,
To mourn old Khayyàm: 'Hail, cheer, and farewell!
You took from death All that life could borrow.'

Fleeting Time vanishes, e'er the winged prize
That flies in its perpetual sunrise.
With the breath of eternity on its lips,
The Bird of Time is All that never dies.

In Naishàpùr, Persia, rose gardens sing,
Then shed their blossoms at the end of spring.
Likewise, Old Khayyàm's Earthly splendor flew;
Yet, his Bird of Time still thrives, on the wing.

— Epilogue —

THE RETURN

In the darkness I alit from the Wiz,
And tried to make sense of this world of His.
I soon found the 'answer' to life's dark quiz:
One must live this life by what light there is.

Oh, never has there been a time more rare,
But that I could truly say, 'I was there
On that Heavenly sphere of blue and green;
Yes, I was there, in life extraordinaire!'

At first, it was like a moving picture show,
Attended by mysteries, row upon row,
That were faceless, laughing, in the dark below,
So I laughed too, and better enjoyed it so.

In the night lies the healthy breath of morn;
The giant oak sleeps within the acorn;
The flower waits for spring inside the seed;
So too in a daydream is one's life born.

Daydreams are filled with thoughts on promenade:
Wishes, fantasies o'er the mind cascade.
Listen well to these plans already made,
For by sundown the phantom shapes may fade.

PRELUDE TO A HOPEFUL DREAM

(The following 17 quatrains are by Positor)

The summer sun with mellow mien retires
Beneath the line of far ecstatic spires;
The evening and the star-blessed night will bring
Transcendent thoughts and amorous desires.

Across the plain fly hosts of silent geese,
Their stridor muted by celestial peace;
For in the midnight haunts of hedonists
The irksome peals of daily strife must cease.

The lake is calm, the stellar gaze benign;
The gibbous moon marks out the bay's smooth line.
High-leaping fish and iridescent birds
In chorus serenade the sacred vine.

The moonlit mermaids by the waterfall,
The sentries on the distant city wall,
The barrel-bearers and the servant boys—
A graceful aura lingers round them all.

Behold the Magus at his nightly feast:
The very synthesis of god and beast!
Some montane maiden or riparian nymph
Inspires the musings of this pleasure-priest.

He plucks sweet cherries from a scented bowl
While waves of wisdom animate his soul;
He ponders things exalted and profane—
Love, music, and Creation's final Goal.

THE SWEET LAND OF THE FREE

Come, ye who languish in some frosty clime,
Or fret morosely in a peaceless time,
Let thought of cold or conflict now recede;
Imbibe with me a draught of the sublime.

I know a land where every stone is sweet;
Kind breezes vie to soften summer's heat,
The noon is gentle as the dusk or dawn,
And songs resound from each contented street.

When, after work in garden, road, or square,
Discerning folk to tree-lined yards repair
With fragrant wine to elevate the soul,
They sit and argue World and Spirit there.

Some speak about a realm beyond the sky,
Where God determines how we live and die.
Such pious words with distant mantras blend;
'Tis vain to challenge Destiny, they sigh.

But men of action, with emphatic voice,
Assert the truth of human will and choice:
Experience reveals no Deity,
So let us cast off doctrine and rejoice.

Astrologers unfold their ancient charts
That carve the Cosmos into rigid parts,
But keen observers indicate the flaws
Of strict reliance on unchanging arts.

They talk of final and initial states,
Which Science probes, and Theory adumbrates,
While Logic prunes the fancy's fecund tree
And frees the mind from dogma's dismal straits.

One thinker ventures: 'All must needs begin',
But others note the fallacy therein:
A Universe arising from a Void
Needs non-existence for its origin!

Discussion turns to arithmetic themes,
And plans for novel calculation schemes:
The Zero, and the Negative, and Root,
Which occupy an innovator's dreams.

The puzzle of the genesis of Man,
The magnitude of Time's historic span,
The stuff of stars, the levity of light,
All pass within the conversation's scan.

The talk persists, the evening hours advance,
Attendants pour, and comely maidens dance,
Till wine, love, beauty, and enlightenment
Induce in all a deep ecstatic trance.

— Rubaiyat Related Themes —

**THE FIND OF THE RUBAIYAT EDITION
KNOWN AS THE 'GREAT OMAR'**

**(Notation is not applicable here
in this section by Austin.)**

**The 'Great Omar' jewel-encrusted edition
Of the *Rubaiyat* had but two renditions,
But one of them was destroyed in conflict,
And the other went down with the Titanic.**

**It's presently lost in my basement lair,
As I know it's down there, somewhere,
For I scanned some images from it there.**

***The lone jewel encrusted 'Great Omar',
Now worth over 20 million dollars,
Sunk, with the mighty Titanic.
I plucked it up from the North Atlantic.***

**The book has 1,051 semiprecious stones,
Set in 18-carat gold, many in the cover alone,
5,000 separate pieces of collared leathers,
And 100 square feet of 22-carat feathered
Gold leaf in the tooling and the edges weathered.**

**It had been purchased by a Jewish investor
In New York City, over a century ago, and more.**

***It went down, down, the sounds whirling around,
When the ice broke through the Titanic's crown.***

**Vivid illustrations by Elihu Vedder's artistry
Adorn the passages of metaphysical poetry,
But the most compelling aspect of the book
Is its ornate binding—two years it took.**

It is bound in morocco leather fine
And inlaid with a peacock design,
Beneath elaborate arches, exotically
Engulfed by a flowing grape vine tree.

Its cover is implanted with precious stones,
Including rubies, garnets, topaz, and amethysts,
And emeralds, each stone set in 18-carat gold.

It is a magnificent masterpiece of its kind,
With three peacocks in the heart of its bind,
Surrounded by vine sprays, a snake in an apple tree,
Roses and poppies, with the whole worked within
In leather and jewels, amid the verse pearls' wisdom.

250 amethysts form the bunches of grapes,
And the decorative ground is pure gold scape.

Down it went, into the black, watery abysm,
Resting there for a hundred years in its prison.

The specters of death and life's impermanence
Permeate Omar's quatrains, which themes thence
Are reflected in the tooling of the jeweled Rubaiyat,
Carried out by the firm of Sangorski and Sutcliffe.

Their front cover features a resplendent peacock motif,
While the inside back cover centralizes the bony skull.

Unlike the vaunted dead aboard the Titanic,
The name of the great book lives on and on.

Phoenix-like, the glorious peacock spreads
His lustrous plumage through the years,
In further irony and emulation of Khayyam.

Down, down, its spell was treasured for thee alone.

...

My uncle was finishing up on a Titanic Deep Sea
Documentary, in 1987, and had thus invited me
To the site, after principal photography
And filming had been wrapped completely.

We sent the robot probe down for one last peep,
On a special mission, into the depths of the deep,
Where the veiled lightning slept, in its lonely keep.

We viewed the wreck remotely, on a monitor;
We saw death and decay sleeping everywhere.

The probe entered a gaping hole in the hull,
And we directed it toward the specie room,
The place reserved for the more expensive,
Secret, or official parcels crossing the Atlantic.

Down, down, we are the bright form beside thee.

The probe's beam lit the way as we guided it
By referring to a map of the mighty ship.

In time, we found a secure metal box, #14,
And grabbed it with the probe's robot arm,
Then carefully backed out the hearty probe,
Though the ship, and on up to the surface.

The box was water tight, the rust sealing it more.
We cut through the lid, and there it brightly shone;
We had the one and only copy of the 'Great Omar'.

Perhaps there was some extended discussion
Of literary treasures at dinner on the Titanic
On the fateful Sunday night of April 14, 1912,
Which sumptuous feast was hosted by the Widners,

For Captain Smith was there, and a few more,
Alongside the bibliophile, Harry Wilkins Widner,

Who was bringing home many a festive jewel
To festoon his already impressive collection.

The ocean liner had sunk like a stone in the dark,
After the iceberg had sliced all of its compartments,
Rousing the world to the nature of this fragile life.

Down, down, as the moth flies into the flame.

That the *Rubaiyat* had gone down with the Titanic
Is all to do with the transience of human existence.

Omar Khayyam went down in 1123,
And with him went a gifted philosopher,
Mathematician, celestial observer, and poet.

Down, down, as the bottom draws the stone,
Where death reigns over all that are known.

Khayyam was born of humble origins;
His surname means 'tentmaker',
But he rose to a life of study,
Under the benevolence of the Sultan
In what is present-day Iran.

Thus he could turn to treatises
On algebra, on metaphysics,
And Euclidean geometry.

The Rubáiyát Publisher's Gem

These pearls of thought in Persian gulfs were bred,
Each softly lucent as a rounded moon;
The diver Omar picked them from their bed,
Fitzgerald strung them on an English thread.

THE SECRET LIFE OF OMAR'S RUBAIYAT POEMS

The secrets which my book of love has bred,
Cannot be told for fear of loss of head;
Since none is fit to learn, or cares to know,
'Tis better all my thoughts remain unsaid.

There are fatwas against rationalists;
Shariah has become the supreme truth,
Once venerated figures are heretics;
The intellectual sciences are forbidden.

I'm forced to play the game of pretending
To be a good Muslim; even went to Mecca.

Of secrets of the world, my book defined
For fear of malice should not be outlined;
Since none here worthy are amongst the dolts,
I can't reveal the thoughts that crowd my mind.

Even teaching is prohibited.
Libraries are no longer supported.
It's safer for one to write on science
And mathematics than philosophy.

My poems are inwardly like snakes who bite
The Shariah and are chains and restraints.
Some I get away with because of the
Poetic mode of expression I have adopted.

There is no benefit in the science of medicine,
And no truth lies in the science of geometry,
Logical and natural sciences are heretical
And those practicing them are heathens.

The promise of reward and punishment
And the quandary of bodily resurrection

Derails one's attention, diverting it from
The here and now, where one should be focused.

The whole problem is that 'God' is not
Established, yet I grant the possibility,
Upgrading the notion to a 'maybe';
But they still preach it as a surety!

Ghazzali studied with me for some years
And came to my home in the morning,
'Fore he could be seen—religiously torn;
So I had a drum beaten on my roof.

Ye do not grasp the truth but still ye grope;
Why waste then life and sit in doubtful hope.
Beware! And hold forever Holy Name
From torpor sane or sot in death will slope.

Some strung the pearls of thought by searching deep,
And told some tales about Him—sold them cheap;
But none has caught a clue to secret realms,
They cast a horoscope and fall asleep.

Had I but over the heavens control
I'd remove this bullish ball beyond the goal
And forthwith furnish better worlds and times
Where love will cling to every freeman's soul.

I wonder if 'Lord' could change the world
Just so that I may see his plans unfurled.
Would he remove my name from roll of call?
Or would my dish with larger sops be hurled?

Since mortal compositions are cast by Hand Divine,
Why then the flaws that throw them out of line?
If formed sublime, why must He shatter them?
If not, to whom should we the fault assign?

Anon! The pious people would advise,
That as we die, we rise up fools or wise.
'Tis for this cause we keep with lover and wine,
For in the end with same we hope to rise.

In Paradise are angels, as men trow
And fountains with pure wine and honey flow.
If these be lawful in the world to come
May I not love the like down here below?

This ruthless Wheel that makes so great a show,
Unravels no one's knot, shares no one's woe;
But when it sights a wounded, weary heart,
It hurries on to strike another blow.

And those who show their prayer-rugs are but mules—
Mere hypocrites who use those rugs as tools;
Behind the veil of zealotry they trade,
Trading Islam—worse than heathen are those fools.

If justice ruled the working of the heavens,
All the affairs of Men would prosper well,
If sciences guided all our worldly acts,
Who would be sorry for the men of science.

Serve only the wise if and when you find.
Let fast and prayer blast, you need not mind,
But listen to truth from what Omar Khayyam says:
Drink wine, steal if you must, but be ever kind.

If ye would love, be sober, wise and cool
And keep your mind and senses under rule.
If ye desire your drinking be loved by All;
Injure no person, never act a fool.

Those strong in virtue and of learning deep,
Whose merits joined lights for their fellows keep
Have found no way out of this darksome night,
They've told their tale, and then gone back to sleep.

Upon that day when sundered is the sky.
And darkened is the stars' bright galaxy.
Upon the plain I'll seize Thy skirt and cry,
"For what sin, Idol, doom'st Thou me to die?"
...
The Eternal has to be everything,
Superimposed, not a certain pathing;
It can't have inputs, with no beginning;
So, what chose the song our universe sings?

The Eternal is as a multiverse,
Potentially, with no information,
As in Bable's Library of all books,
Being as useless as Nothing's zero.

...

A flower is life, but in time that flies.
It buds, blooms and dies right before our eyes.
It's a lesson to learn in beauty's form;
Yes, we are the rose, in different guise.
(—Jennifer)

What's here now has to be as that long before,
Not new out of the blue, for there is no more;
So, we and all are akin to what is,
Not less—we're united beyond the door.

Dreams are the starlight of our minds,
A canopy of hope that shines
Above our lives to light our days,
And prove we are more than our daily ways.
(—Jennifer)

ON POETRY

Long time, old friend, since you lived and died,
Yet you taught us wisdom by the fireside,
Led me and mine along the riverside,
And watered our flowers through the springtide.

You live forever, through your words, a poem
Of life, a conscious dream, an immortal gem.
When we read it, the verses come to life—
In living out your words we must know them.

Saturate the mind with every quatrain,
Till your life's good deeds echo each refrain,
Till all philosophies are embedded,
Till dream, wish, and life are one and the same.

I have ended up writing poems in the styles
Of Shelley's and Old Khayyàm's wiles,
The former being flowingly lyrical—
The latter twistingly epigrammatical.

A poem is both the thought and the presence,
An object born from the profoundest sense,
An image of diction, feeling, and rhythm;
We're both the existence and the essence.

A poem is a truth fleshed in living words,
Which by showing unapprehended proof
Lifts the veil to reveal hidden beauty:
It's life's image drawn in eternal truth.

Poetry makes immortal what is best
In life: it frees images of dreams impressed,
Apprehends the vanishing phantasms,
And sends them forth in fine words, fully dressed.

Poems echo the soul's vocabulary,
Being just a shadow of what's primary;
But, once ideas have been fully grasped,
Mere words are no longer necessary.

Poems are renderings of the soul's spirit,
The highest power of language and wit.
The reader then translates back to spirit;
If the soul responds, then a poem you've writ!

Art and poetry enrich human experience,
But they're no substitutes for the living of it.
Like the figures on an urn, should we live life less?
No, because what is deathless is also lifeless!

EXTRA QUATRAINS

Night's mystical flight of fulfilled desires
Heralds the day-star, as darkness retires;
The Sun subsumes the stars, fire-paints the dawn,
And captures the Sultan's holy spires.

Breathe in all that's good, breathe out all that's bad;
Peace flows into you—it's warm, wet, and glad.
Feel it spread throughout the body, then say,
'This is the best life that I've ever had!'

I flew here, as a bird from the wild, in aim
Up to a higher nest my course to frame;
But, finding here no guide who knows the way,
Fly out by the same door where through I came.

What would be the price of a moment's breath
Purchased from Death's hand at the final hour?
All the world's wealth cannot extend the power
That drains the cup and withers the flower.

Maybe this, maybe that, of a 'God',
On and on, of worn ideas long trod,
Trying to show nature's not what it does,
Spouting this and that—dust into the sod.

They bless the 'needed' soul with the holy kiss
Of life, being this of which to replace us with;
For what did natural selection ever do, in vain,
Spending so extravagantly on the higher brain?

Heart-flight is love that the wondrous Earth brings,
As wind to the soul whispers unimaged things;
Senses merge, as streams, to flow beyond joy;
Imagination fires enlightened wings.

The energy of eternity is our maternity.
We find ourselves lost, really, here without asking...
But eventually, aft the lost-and-found,
The karma overruns the dogma into the ground.

There is no answer given, but only
A larger mystery of the One and Only,
Which is an infinitely larger question there,
Rendering the entire 'answer' beyond repair.

This wheel of heaven, which makes us all afraid,
I liken to a lamp's revolving shade,
The sun the candlestick, the earth the shade,
And men the trembling forms thereon portrayed.

Hence old or sick, one might regret or pine,
Giving all to have back some better time.
Now you are young and fine, so be glad, shine;
Ne'er again will you live this life of thine.

We, of the endless forms most beautiful,
Are stunned that our glass to the brim is full,
Life's wine coursing through us, as 'magical',
On this lovely, rolling sphere so bountiful.

For once we were, our presence full beheld
Spirit, body, heart, and mind, so, in meld,
As more than the parts we became the whole—
Human beings living lives unparalleled.

There are no sins, but just destiny's fate,
Which even includes one's learnings of late.
We and all are but whirl-pools, of the one oscillation,
Some lasting longer, yes, but of the same instantiation.

What providence determines our destiny plucked?
Is it the stars, by chance, that rain down luck,
Or is it just serendipity and good fortune
Created by our own karma of kismet done?

A diamond sparkles though its every face,
Each plane contributing a view of space.
Such radiant richness does life reflect,
For one facet does not a diamond make.

Life must be more like a mosaic done,
Than a focused laser tunnel of sun.
Since few lengthy pleasures are lent to us,
We build stained-glass windows of small ones.

Like the bright faces that define the jewel
Friends enrich each others view of life's gem:
As love's reflection in life's diamond, they're
Glints and gleams of reality's sparkle.

They tried to undo evolution's pace of snails,
But the stratified fossils ever told the tales
Of no special humans at once unveiled
But of only natural selection's weathered sails.

Which of the following is more worthwhile:
The rainbow or the gold under its smile?
Well, the rainbow is here and now; the pot
May not turn out to be worth the miles.

God thought of, planned, designed, and implemented
Human Nature—angelic to demented,
And in His recipe's span those expressed
Unsurprisingly had to be reinvented.

Shirking responsibility, the Blamer
Cited humans as the culprits of his err,
And cast them out of Eden, to this day—
This evil being God's own Original Sin.

The Father Notion they based on themselves,
As the best answer that was ever delved:
The demanding Male Mind who was called 'God',
An idea for some to this day, well trod.

Answers were needed for them to persist:
They extended the Notion with more myths
And legends into lore layered upon,
Inventing all the scrolls of scripture on.

'God' brought both fear and comfort in those days,
Making people better through fearsome ways,
Although worse for some—the unchosen tribes,
Protecting their notions, as taught by scribes.

A wasteland of superstition plod,
Instantiates a meaning for 'God'.
Emotion e'er sets up a firm blockade
When thoughts fired more build a stockade.

If we're captives of a lifeless day,
A wall around us, brick by brick, will weigh.
Habited we'll stay, until, one day,
Bricks will be moulded from our dusty clay.

Hopes flitter and flutter like butterflies—
Whose forms show there can be a second guise,
Although still one chained to time's sovernty.
We cannot fly through time's skies two-way wise.

Push forward, and deeper, beyond your fears;
We guide thee, we lift thee, we dry your tears;
We're illumination beside thee—of
The Spirits Of Unconditional Love.

Be happy! For the moon of thy festival will come,
The means of mirth will all be propitious;
This moon has become lean, bent-figured, and thin,
Thou may'st say that it will sink under this trouble.

Enjoy the play that you get to act in,
Sometimes retreating to the back row,
In the distanced audience, witnessing afar,
Finding peace and lasting gladness there.

Luckily, we live at peak, atop life's pile
Of miraculous lives from eons of wiles.
We're alive, thanks to all who've come before,
So, how can we live by any style but 'smile'?

Mind is the ultimate of all there is;
It is the universe: billions of years
Of primordial material, complex."
So, then, what more could human beings want?

A life ought to be rich with excitation—
One wishes to enjoy complete sensation.
Pleasure's not merely a reward for working;
It's life's foremost experience of elation.

As of now I hold reality's attention;
This is the time of my present comprehension.
What is past exists only in my memory,
The future only in my imagination.

Dying in the shadow of the minaret,
Old Khayyàm faces death without regret.
The Bird of Time lands; evening winds murmur;
Omar savors the glow of his last sunset.

THE TRANSMOGRIFICATION FROM THE FARSI ARABIC

(In this section by Austin, the female voice is in italics and the male voice is in regular.)

**FitzGerald's transmogrification
Of Omar's quatrains into Victorian English
And his reordering of them into a Persian ecolog,
Is primary among the rare conjunctions
That made for the greatest poem in history.**

**Rather than recounting the word by word details
Of the Persia-fumed inspirations coalescing
Into FitzGerald's inspired improvements
And rearrangements here, a poetic,
Analogous kind of description is presented.**

The Book of Quatrains

**While writing, much more is drawn from the mind
For there is relative silence, with no starting gun,
As in speaking, for it is in real time done.
The muses sing, of one's own depths mined.**

***It says on the cover that 'fumes' therein
Have escaped from an interment within,
That it shall take the passerby unaware.***
Oh, I'm already affected by it! Lay here.

***The scent's name is printed on the label
And is called 'Omar's Enchantment', that's all.***
**It's delightful. I savor what it supposes.
It's a mixture of incense, wine, and roses.**

***It's some sort of an elixir of time.
It well composes, potent and sublime.***
**It also has hints of sandalwood, jasmine,
Lotus, and bits of golden saffron fine.**

Now, for the golden verse, as the first.
For its olden age, it is none the worse.
Although day-tide has just barely spoken,
I no less will open our precious token,

This mystery book of poetry sealed,
With waxen shield, it having been concealed
For hundreds of years in the secret chamber
Of the old monastery's remainder.

Ope it as one would a tender lover.
A bottle's encased inside the cover.
Its spirit's mist apparently escaped
As our fuminous volume was undraped.

I'm captivated by the Persia fumes.
As I. It's the perfume of ageless rhymes,
From those grand, learnéd Sufi looms of time.
We'll have to learn how to read between the lines.

The tome is written in foreign language,
In fine verses of thirteen syllables,
Epigrammatic, in four-line stanzas,
It having many swirlas and circulas.

It's written in middle Persian, I've looked,
Having handled many such foreign books—
My editor's role in the abbey's nooks;
I thought to hide it in one of the rooks.

The library's most valuable book!
For I've illuminated and unhooked
Many of the monastery's great books.
For it a long and joyous month I took.

It was the only writing I could save,
Yet it's the only book we'll ever crave.

What are you, old work? she asks of the book.
I add, Are you alive? By you I shook.
The book replies, "I am the book of life—
Pages rife with the antidotes of strife;

"I'm a truth, a living philosophy.
I live forever through my words, wholly.
On my pages are found man's joys, follies,
Sorrows, wisdom, and all of his jollies.

"Read me and my ideas will come alive,
Demonstrating the best ways to survive!
It is by experiencing my words
That you shall know them, backwards and forwards."

We look long at the now quieted tome,
Deeply inhaling its heady perfume.
Oh, that heavenly, earthly scent, she sighs.
Oh, book of quatrains, you are Persia-fume!

We watch the book moving about, amazed;
Sparkles and twirls whirl out of the pages.
*It's rising, breathing, and coming to life,
As husband in the presence of his wife.*

Words bounce around; over the page they run,
They often changing into English ones.

*Even whole verses are now roundly dancing—
Of the Arabic worlds—dervishes whirling.
They're trying to settle from the struggle,
But the words do again jump and juggle,*

*Some hanging back, then ever surging forth,
Darting around through the poem's long course,
Then make stanzas, to form a brighter source,
From aspects of the pervading concepts.*

'Tis as if this transmogrification
Is trying to preserve all relation
Of the original schema throughout,
The whole translation process devout,

Including literal means, rhythm, rhyme,
Melody, syllable, meter, and time;
But this doesn't seem to be workative,

And so it follows that something must give,
And this might well sadly be the ration
That is usually lost in translation.

See! Out of that desperation, uncaged,
The verses are jumping right off the page,
Splashing into the bottle of perfume,
Wherein they are redistilling, subsumed.

Now they're leaping back out, onto the page,
Recomposing themselves, for this time—our age,

Whereupon they're condensing, restaging,
Into Victorian verse, over paging—
Original concepts forming new quatrains
In which Omar's meaning's essence remains.

The lines are now ten English syllables,
Rather than the Arabic thirteen quills,
Yet holding even more related meanings,
Heretofore unnoted, yet the verses

Are still in groups of four lines per stanza,
And the correct lines still rhyme, per lingua,
Although some of the ending quatrain schemes
Don't seem to have quite the same rhyming means.

Yes, only the unneeded has been lost;
A charm has been added, the good not tossed;
It is something somehow much better told,
Yet e'er within the spirit of the old.

OMAR'S OTHER WORKS

Nizam al-Mulk invited me to Isfahan,
To opulent palaces, the imperial court.
I read the rich libraries of the Seljuqs,
Which offered Euclid and many treasures.

I worked on the new calendar for Sanjar,
In an astronomical observatory.
The Sultan wanted the first day as Spring,
So I spread the extra days far and wide.

The Persian New Year of Nowrýz is based
On an actual astronomical criterion,
The sun entering the astronomical sign
Of Aries at the vernal equinox.

*This brilliant method guarantees keeping
Nowrýz at the vernal equinox forever.*

15 days were added every 62 years,
The length of a year being 365.241935 days,
And for every 5000 years,
The calendar has to be adjusted by one day.

The years 4, 8, 12, 16, 20, 24, 28,
And 33 became leap years of 366 days
With the average year being 365.2424 days.

Sultan Sanjar had me back to stay at the court.
I worked the division of a quadrant of a circle,
And refuted doubt concerning parallels,
And in algebra related the conic geometry.

On the deception of knowing
The two quantities of gold and silver
In a compound made of the two...

On music theory, of mathematical relationship
Among notes, minor, major, and tetrachords.

Made references to the views of Farabi and Avicenna
To offer a reclassification of musical scales.

A discussion regarding the relationships
Among time, motion, and God,
Which ends with an Avicennian discussion
On incorporeal substances, celestial spheres
And their relationship to angels.

The essence of The Necessary is One
In all aspects and in no case can there
Be multiplicity except in abstraction,
In which case its number can reach infinity.

The essence for which multiplicity
In abstraction is conceived does not become multiple.
All of the attributes of the Necessary Being
Are abstract and none of them contains any existence.

Good Has to Include Evil as its Opposite:

If one were to conduct a good versus evil
'Cost-benefit analysis,'
The good far exceeds the evil.

The ratio between the goodness that darkness brings
To the evil it causes exceeds that of one to a million,

And in accordance with wisdom in the world,
There is very little evil
That is qualitatively or quantitatively
Comparable with good.

In my major philosophical work,
On Being and Necessity:

'Avoiding a great amount of good
Due to the necessity of having little evil
Is itself a great deal of evil.'

'Why is there something rather than nothing?

Being is better than non-being,
The very gift of existence is ontologically good
And the world has been created for a good purpose.

The question of 'being' and 'necessity'
Are among the most
Perplexing philosophical questions.

First ontological questions are concerned with
'What is.'

Second, the question concerning
'What is it?'

Which pertains to the substance or essence of a thing;

Third,
'Why is it?'

This last question seeks
To determine the cause of a thing.

On the necessity of contradiction in the world,
Determinism and subsistence.

On the relationship between
Existent beings and existence,

The accidental relationship between them
And whether either of them exist by their own necessity.

On the knowledge of the universal principles
Of existence and the universals of knowledge.

AUSTIN'S NEW CALENDAR

The last truly major revision to the calendar occurred over eight hundred years ago, when Omar Khayyàm realigned the Moslem calendar so that the seasons would arrive at the same time each year. Back then the year started in March, with the spring, the more logical time for a new year to start, I would say, since nature is new in the spring. It took Europe a long time to pick up on the changes. I suppose they got tired of celebrating Christmas in July-type weather or shoveling snow in the summertime.

Omar also revised his philosophic calendar to suit his mental outlook, by advocating that dead yesterday and unborn tomorrow be removed from the calendar; thus, he could truly live for Today. Later on, he refined this theory further by also removing dead and unborn minutes, so that he could live for the moment. My calendar revisions are more along those lines.

So, it's high time for another major revision to the calendar, one that's reflective of modern times, for the only improvements made during the last few hundred years have been to skip leap days in years that are evenly divisible by 400, and, more recently, to add a few insignificant leap-seconds every few year or so ("Wow, that seemed like a really long weekend!").

First of all, I am eliminating the months of January (Bran-new-airy), February (Feb-buries), and March (March!) because, 1) They all contain cold and rotten weather, and 2) They totally lack holidays on which we could get time off with pay from work. It's a heck of a long wait for a holiday between New Year's Day and Memorial Day (we used to get Good Friday off, but now even that day has been eliminated, for it's a religious-ethnic holiday and other religious-ethnic groups could then have proposed other such holidays, and so there'd be no time left for actual work days). Note: don't worry, Valentine's Day is being retained and moved elsewhere, as is New Year's Day.

I am adding a whole new month, called Remember, which comes right after December. That way you will have some extra time to do all of the things that you meant or forgot to do during the year. Just think, there will be not as much need to say "Wait until next year!".

My revised year starts in the spring, in April, which, as I've said, is much more appropriate, since it is a time for renewal and rebirth. By the way, it is easily proved that the year once started in spring by noting the Latin numbers from which the months got their modern names, i.e., 7-sept, 8-oct, 9-nov, 10-dec. We, of course, have now adopted these Latin numeric prefixes into general English, as well, for example, septuagenarian (age 70-80), octagon (8-sided), octave (8 musical degrees), novena (9 days of devotion), decimal (base 10), decimate (to kill one in ten), decathlon, decade, etc.

I also discovered that the old names of July and August were Quintus (Latin 5) and Sextus (Latin 6), but Julius and Augustus Caesar changed the names to suit their own. As for May, June, and April, those were the names of the Caesars' girlfriends. So, anyway, what all this means is that since December used to be the tenth month (dec), the year obviously once started in March. I am generally readopting this policy, except that, since I've eliminated March, my revised year must now start in April, on April's Fools Day, in fact, which will have to share the honor with New Year's Day, an appropriate combination considering all of the foolish things that we do on New Year's Eve.

So, since my year as so far constructed is only ten months long, I must now distribute the excess days that made up the two missing months. I would like to make all the months thirty days long, since people have problems with the current variations. So, I am introducing a new, unnumbered day into the week, called Funday, a day which does not have to be numbered or accounted for in any way whatsoever.

Funday occurs between Sunday and Monday. On Funday you can do as you please. Funday doesn't even have a numerical date, and so it cannot possibly count against schedules, deadlines, or bills. Weekends, as we all know, have always been too short, but now, with the introduction of Funday, weekends become three days long.

I have, as have many others, already pioneered the concept that led to Funday: I get up late on Saturday and Sunday to recover energy spent during the work week, and then, by Sunday night, being so well rested, I go to sleep quite late or sometimes not at all and stay up all night reading or doing you know what. Of course, I pay for all of this by being very tired on Monday, but naturally it's much better to be tired on company time than on your own time, and who ever expects much of Monday anyway.

So, this is what led me to the idea of a Funday on which you could do whatever you want; you don't even have to visit your relatives. Funday is totally dedicated to fun, and a new law will make it a crime for you to do anything else, although shopping and home chores are allowed if you whistle while you work or sing a happy song. Yes, people are so harried these days that we have to force them to enjoy life.

So, thanks to Funday there will be no more rush-rush orhectic feelings when the work week starts. People need no longer waste short weekends of great weather by doing silly things like going grocery shopping or doing the laundry.

Well, you might say, instead of lengthening the week why not just get people to do all their weekend chores during the week, but, of course, they can't, since they're so stressed out and exhausted when they get home from work that they just collapse and can't even do the simplest thing.

Yes, I know that this is simply a matter of attitude and style, but, believe me, personal changes, even such common sense changes, seem to take huge amounts of effort; whereas, I can solve the problem more easily with the introduction of Funday.

But, ten months of thirty numbered days plus five undated Fundays each month equals only 350 days, so there are still fifteen more days that must be dispersed into the new calendar. I am solving this by adding a special summer and winter festival period of seven days each, the winter festival being no more really than a re-establishment of the old Saturnalian pagan festival held in olden times, before the Christians put a damper on it. This winter festival is added between Christmas and New Year's Day so that we can have a vacation from our vacation of visiting relatives and feasting and pigging out. The summer festival is inserted between July and August, and centers around the true midsummer's day. Naturally these festivals do not count against anyone's vacation time.

There are just a few minor alterations left. There is still one day left to be accounted for, and I am inserting it between May and June as Valentines Day. I am removing a day from June, so that the saying "Nothing is so rare as a day in June" will actually be true. In the old calendar, a day in February was 4.2% more rare than a day of June, but, of course, February is gone now. The day removed from June will be called World Day. On this day we should try to get all the world's peoples to coexist in perfect harmony. This day occurs between June and July. I am moving the Fourth of July holiday to the first Monday in July so that we will have yet another extra long weekend.

Monday mornings and Friday afternoons are to be designated as home/work transition adjustment-recovery periods, during which one need not be present at work, thus reducing the work week to only four days!

Yes, the computer age has arrived and it's time that we reaped its benefits and gained more leisure time, for this was the promise of the computer age: that computers would free us, so why do I feel like they have become our masters?

Furthermore, the nebulous day called Someday is being removed from the calendar and from everyday conversation, because what it really meant was "Noneday", as in "Someday we'll go out to lunch".

Also, just as a matter of information, note that the days of the week were named after the sun, the moon, and all of the known planets of the time, although some of the days derive their names from French or Latin: Sunday (sun), Monday (moon), Tuesday (Mardi in French, or Mars), Wednesday (Mercredi, or Mercury in French), Thursday (Jeudi in French, or Jupiter), Friday (Vendredi in French for Venus), Saturday (Saturn). However, this still leaves Pluto, Uranus, and Neptune unrepresented, but I'll probably leave those for my next revision.

My new names for the days of the week are: Onesday, Twosday, Wedsday, Thirstday, Fryday, Satday, Sundae, and Funday, and are for, respectively, self, relationships, marrieds, drinking, frying fish, sitting around, ice cream and fudge, and fun. During pandemics, everyday is Blursday.

Or, we could just forget all of these revisions and go back to Omar's great idea about having a calendar with only one day on it: Today.

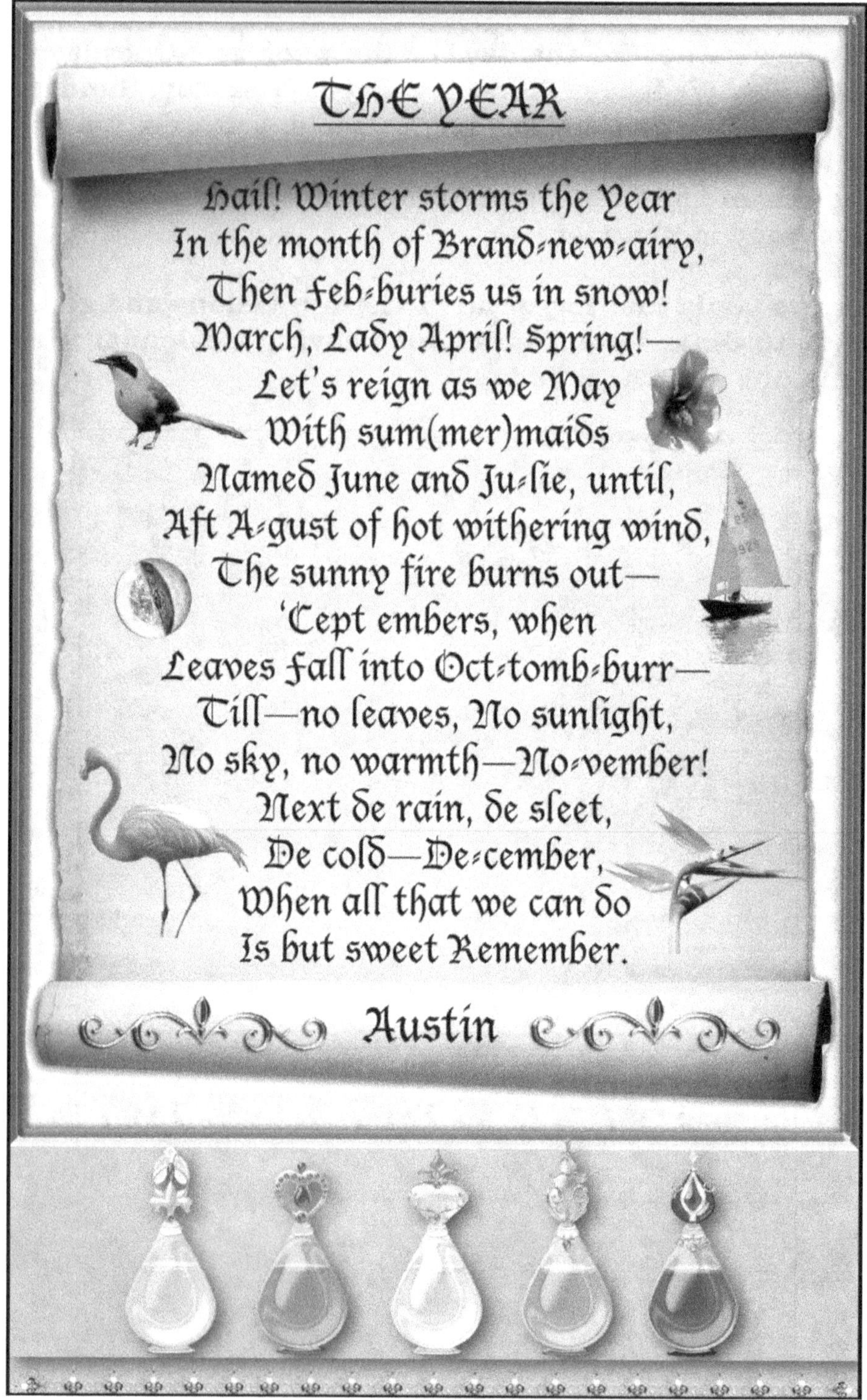

THE YEAR

Hail! Winter storms the Year
In the month of Brand-new-airy,
Then Feb-buries us in snow!
March, Lady April! Spring!—
Let's reign as we May
With sum(mer)maids
Named June and Ju-lie, until,
Aft A-gust of hot withering wind,
The sunny fire burns out—
'Cept embers, when
Leaves fall into Oct-tomb-burr—
Till—no leaves, No sunlight,
No sky, no warmth—No-vember!
Next de rain, de sleet,
De cold—De-cember,
When all that we can do
Is but sweet Remember.

Austin

THE ANSWERS TO EVERYTHING

On What 'IS'

(Particles as the energy excitations of quantum fields)

An Eternal Basis has to be so,
For a lack of anything cannot sow,
Forcing there to be something permanent,
As partless, from which composites can grow.

There can't be other directions given,
To that which no start; it is undriven;
So, it is as Everything possible,
Either as linear or as all at once.

Consider quantum fields of waves atop
One another: waves are continuous,
And so qualifiy as Fundamental;
Quantized lumps make 'particles', then more.

The temp-forms last from unit charge or strength;
The Basis is coterminal with them,
But is not cosubstantial with the 'things';
The information content is the same as Null!

Note that there is no other absolute:
Newton's fixed space and time got Einstein's boot;
Particle spigots making fields went mute;
Classic fields had no fundamental loot.

... proposed ...

There are no 'if nots' for happened events;
That would be a fantasy world but meant
For simulations and playing mind games—
No use entertaining real replacements.

TOE
The Holy Grail

ON CONSCIOUSNESS

What the meaning to this play we're befit,
From dirt to dust within the script that's writ?
The wise in search have thrown themselves to waste;
Experience alone is the benefit.

Physics describes but the extrinsic causes,
While consciousness exists just for itself,
As the intrinsic, compositional,
Informational, whole, and exclusive—

As the distinctions toward survival,
Though causing nothing except in itself,
As in ne'er doing but only as being,
Leaving intelligence for the doing.

The posterior cortex holds correlates,
For this is the only brain region that
Can't be removed for one to still retain
Consciousness, it having feedback in it;

Thusly, it forms an irreducible Whole,
And this Whole forms consciousness directly,
A process fundamental in nature,
Or's the brain's private symbolic language.

The Whole can also be well spoken of
To communicate with others, as well as
Globally informing other brain states,
For nonconscious parts know not what's being made.
. . .
Oh, those imaginings of what can't be!"
Such as Nought, Stillness, and Infinity,
As well as Apart, Beginning, and End,
Originality, Free Will, and He.

TAMAN SHUD

"And those who Husbanded
the Golden Grain -- OMAR

OMAR
TURKISH BLEND
CIGARETTES
EXCEPTIONAL QUALITY
THE AMERICAN TOBACCO CO
OMAR

OMAR
Turkish Blend
CIGARETTES

When Kipling wrote "East is East, and
West is West, and never the twain shall meet," OMAR
had not been produced. For East and West do meet in OMAR
—meet and mingle their choicest tobaccos in the one Perfect
Turkish Blend—a cigarette for all the world to enjoy.

Cavalla, Ephesus, Mahala, in the picturesque Orient, send
their finest crops, exquisite in flavor and aroma, to unite with
America's sparkling mellowest leaf. The result is a revelation
to smokers of all-Turkish and blended cigarettes—a new, re-
freshing, exhilarating smoke, full of snap, zest and relish, enjoy-
able beyond comparison.

20 for 15c

THE AMERICAN TOBACCO COMPANY